Cycling
for Fitness

Dave Smith

A & C Black • London

Thanks to

Carmel for putting up with me while I wrote this book.
Jemimah and Solomon for distracting me while I tried to write this book
'Computer Mark' for saving my hard disk.
God, for inventing legs, knowing full well that we'd need them one day to
ride bikes.

Published in 2001 by A & C Black (Publishers) Ltd
35 Bedford Row, London WC1R 4JH

ISBN 0 7136 5140 7

A CIP catalogue record for this book is available from the British Library.

Note: Whilst every effort has been made to ensure that the content of this book is as technically accurate and as sound as possible, neither the authors nor the publishers can accept responsibility for any injury or loss sustained as a result of the use of this material.

Acknowledgements
Cover photograph courtesy of Jump, Hamburg.
Line illustrations on pages 27, 28, 29, 30, 42, 44, 45, 58 and 96 by Dave Saunders.
All others by Jean Ashley.
Photographs on page 38 courtesy of Polar heart rate monitors; page 17 courtesy of Pulse Fitness; pages 12, 18, 20, 21, 31 and 36 courtesy of Specialized UK; pages 2, 19, 22, 34, 46, 48, 49, 50, 80, 122, 124 and 125 courtesy of Stockfile.

Typeset in 10/12pt Minion Display

Printed and bound in Great Britain by Biddles Ltd, Guildford and Kings Lynn

Contents

Preface

Cycling is a sport of equality, available to men, women and children alike. It need not be expensive, and under medical advice and supervision, it need not exclude the elderly, disabled or infirm. On top of this, of course, cycling offers a pleasurable and efficient means of transport.

Many people find cycling an enjoyable means of improving both their fitness and their health without the injury risks associated with 'weight-bearing' activities such as running. Even if you are a complete newcomer to cycling you will experience positive 'training' effects within days of commencing a regular training programme.

The aim of this book is to provide practical and accessible information for both the beginner and the already-practising cyclist – helping you to understand the complete range of benefits offered by the humble bicycle.

Using this book

Cycling for Fitness is intended primarily for the novice and the less experienced rider. Its structure guides you through from the very beginning: Part I explains exactly what we mean by the terms 'health' and 'fitness' and how cycling can benefit both. The novice will also find Part II useful for advice on 'getting ready' – choosing and fitting a suitable bike and purchasing the appropriate equipment.

If you are already set up for your chosen cycle activity you can bypass this section, and move on to Part III which deals with riding techniques, general training principles, and specific training patterns and programmes. This section also includes information on nutrition, flexibility and conditioning.

If you wish to move into the competitive sphere, Part IV looks at the different types of cycle sport on offer and examines the fitness demands and training plans specific to each.

Dave Smith
January 2001

Part I
Introduction

① Cycling, health and fitness

Defining health and defining fitness

Given the huge growth of the fitness industry over the past 15 years – and the accompanying growth in understanding of the various processes involved in physical exercise – it is perhaps surprising that many people still confuse the notions of being 'fit' and being 'healthy'.

Health may be defined as an individual's freedom from illness; whereas fitness refers to the ability of an individual to undertake mechanical work, such as lifting and moving objects, efficiently. It is therefore possible to be healthy without being fit, and vice-versa. For example, someone who is free from all signs and symptoms of illness might have a low level of fitness and tire easily when performing physical tasks. Likewise, an experienced cyclist might be very 'fit', yet still suffer from asthma or other such ailments.

However, it is generally accepted that positive changes in fitness levels, achieved through safe and controlled means, can help to protect against ill-health and disease, as well as bringing a wide range of other physical and psychological benefits. This chapter aims to explore these benefits briefly in general terms, moving on to the particular ways in which cycling offers an excellent route to enhanced fitness levels – and therefore, to improved health.

The various components of fitness

The ability to undertake mechanical work is directly related to how well a person has developed what are known as the 'components of fitness'. For example, to move a heavy weight repeatedly, you need the initial strength to pick it up, as well as capability in your muscles to lift the weight time and time again – known as *muscular endurance*.

The components of fitness can be divided into two groups: 'health-related', and 'sports-related'. Health-related components are those which relate to the body's ability to function efficiently when performing everyday tasks (*see* Table 1.1). These include strong healthy lungs, flexibility in your muscles and joints and an appropriate level of body fat. Research indicates that those with good health-related fitness levels will be much less prone to contracting many forms of illness and disease (*see* p. 5). Even those individuals who already suffer from health problems can see an improvement if they follow a controlled exercise programme under medical supervision.

An individual with a high degree of fitness in each of the health-related components shown in Table 1.1, is already in a good position to succeed in many sports – in

Table 1.1 Health-related fitness components

Component	Function
Cardio-respiratory fitness	Efficiency of the lungs, heart and circulatory system – the most important health-related component
Muscular strenth	The force required to move or lift
Muscular endurance	The ability to undertake muscular work repeatedly
Flexibility	The range of movement in muscles and joints
Body composition	The ratio of fat to lean body tissue (muscle)

Table 1.2 Sports-related fitness components

Component	Function
Speed	The ability to move rapidly
Power	The ability to generate force rapidly
Reaction time	The ability to react quickly to things happening around you
Skill	The ability to undertake precise actions co-ordinating the senses (sight, hearing, touch) with muscular movement
Balance	The ability to maintain a stable position while either stationary (static balance) or moving (dynamic balance)

particular, those which involve continuous rhythmic movement and, at least at the recreational level, require only simple skills. Running and cycling are good examples of such sports.

All-round conditioning forms a major part of any athlete's preparation, but there are other components that come into play in achieving sporting excellence. These sports-related components are shown in Table 1.2. A 'sports fit' individual will combine good health-related fitness levels with a highly developed nervous system – responsible for the ability to perform skilled movements, to react at speed, and to produce fast and powerful muscle action.

The concept of physical training

In order to develop any fitness component, it is necessary to train the body. The concept of physical training depends upon the reaction of the human body to the levels of work – or 'stress' – that it experiences. If an office worker undertakes heavy manual work such as gardening, the skin on his or her hands will thicken by way of response to a physical stress not encountered under normal circumstances. The body effectively trains itself to cope. If the work is ceased, the toughened skin will gradually disappear – in a process of 'de-training'.

This general principle applies to physical exercise in all its forms. Cycling is one of the many ways in which the body can be positively stressed, resulting in the development of more efficient physiological systems. According to the American College of Sports Medicine, three brisk 45-minute rides each week – at a pace which has you out of breath, but still able to maintain a conversation – will be adequate for enhancing the cardio-respiratory system, the most important health-related fitness component (*see also* pp. 9–10).

However, in time the body will adapt to such regular, low-level stress; so that the more experienced you become, the more you will have to increase your training levels in order to maintain your fitness gains. This and other key training principles are discussed in detail in Chapter 5.

Exercise and your physical and mental health

When you undertake a programme of regular exercise, you will notice improvements in your basic fitness. However, increasing your activity levels can bring a range of additional, health-related benefits. These can be both physical and psychological.

Physical benefits

There are a number of illnesses that are known as hypokinetic, which means that they are either caused or aggravated by an inactive lifestyle. Obvious examples are heart disease and obesity.

In terms of physical benefits, regular activity can help:

- reduce the risk of dying prematurely, and especially from heart disease

- reduce the risk of developing other diseases such as diabetes and cancer of the colon

- reduce blood pressure in people who already have high blood pressure

- increase metabolic rate, and thus control 'weight' – i.e. reduce body fat

- build and maintain healthy bones, muscles and joints

- boost the immune system, the body's main defence against illness and infection

- improve strength, co-ordination and mobility in older adults[1]

Psychological benefits

Exercise also has many psychological benefits. It has been shown to increase levels of a chemical found in the brain known as monoamine, a mood controller which acts to increase positive thought. Hence the saying that exercise can be a drug! There is also

[1]*Physical Activity and Health: A Report of the Surgeon General,* National Centre for Chronic Disease Prevention and Health Promotion, Altlanta (1999).

some evidence that it can raise levels in the body of a group of chemicals called peptides – in particular, those known as opiate peptides – which are thought to contribute to the 'feel good' factor that often accompanies an especially challenging workout.

The generally accepted psychological benefits of regular exercise are as follows:

- increase in self-confidence, emotional stability and independence

- reduction in anger, anxiety, depression, tension and confusion.

Why choose cycling?

The exercise-induced benefits discussed above are likely to result from most types of activity. So why choose cycling? One answer is that it offers the potential for huge and highly enjoyable variety – from the stationary bike in your local gym or health club, to the relative relaxation of road riding, the challenge and exhilaration of off-road, and the possibility of many different kinds of competitive activity. The different options open to the would-be cyclist are discussed in detail in Chapter 2.

Another, equally important, answer is that recreational cycling – like running and swimming – represents a highly effective form of *aerobic activity*. The term 'aerobic' literally means 'with oxygen', and refers to the chemical pathway in the body which utilises oxygen in order to produce energy.

Exercise and the body's energy production systems

The body's energy production system – or *metabolic* system – provides fuel to the muscles in the form of carbohydrate, fat and protein. Within the muscle, these fuels are converted to a usable energy form known as ATP (adenosine triphosphate). This can happen either aerobically, as described above, using oxygen in the process; or it can happen *anaerobically* – without oxygen. The anaerobic system (metabolism) increases its contribution to energy production when the aerobic system is no longer sufficient to supply total energy requirement. This would typically take place at high training efforts. However, it is the aerobic energy production system that most concerns the newcomer, or the less experienced cyclist, who is training to develop overall fitness.

During aerobic exercise, work is carried out at an intensity that results in the oxygen system providing most of the energy required for muscular contraction. In turn, this helps to develop greater efficiency of the heart, lungs and circulation – known as the *cardio-respiratory system* – and, as discussed above, leads to improved fitness and health. In addition, aerobic work relies on fat as well as carbohydrate, so it can be a useful tool in increasing one's efficiency at burning fat. This 'fat burning effect' is often a key factor motivating an individual's training programme.

By contrast, anaerobic exercise relies purely on carbohydrates and the high energy phosphates for fuel. Carbohydrate is present in the blood as the simple sugar glucose, and is stored in the body as a substance called glycogen which is more compact and quicker to access – especially when needed during a sudden burst of exercise. This is examined in more detail in Chapter 8, *Fuel for fitness*, pp. 105–18.

Exercise and the muscular system – 'under your own steam'

The product of the metabolic system is energy; we now turn to the product of the muscular system, known as *power*.

The unit of power most often used in cycling performance is the *watt*: 1 watt equals 1 joule per second, and is the power needed to move 1 Newton (0.102 kg) over 1 metre in 1 second. In other words, it is the measure of the force being applied to an object, in order to move it (or attempt to move it) over a given distance. When calculating power we must also consider *time* and *energy cost*, or the amount of energy involved in the work.

The following equation is used to calculate average power:

$$\text{average power} = \frac{\text{work done}}{\text{time taken}} = \frac{\text{energy change}}{\text{time taken}}$$

Power (watt) figures have been established for cyclists, with the elite being able to sustain 400 watts for up to 1 hour, and over 2000 watts in explosive efforts lasting less than 2 seconds; a recreational cyclist may achieve 200 watts sustained, and 800 watts of peak power.

The power for cycling is provided mostly by the leg muscles, the main ones at work being the quadriceps and hamstrings in the upper leg, and the gastrocnemius and soleus in the calf. Composed of bunches of long, thread-like muscle fibres, these contract in a sequence that creates the pedalling action. There are actually four types of muscle fibre, although only three need concern us here – the fourth (FT III) being very rare.

Types of muscle fibre

- *Slow twitch*, or slow oxidative – the endurance type. These are the best oxygen burners; they don't tire very easily.

- *Fast twitch*, or fast glycolytic – these are real power fibres, used for all-out speed and power activities such as track sprinting. They can't burn oxygen (they aren't aerobic) and so tire very quickly.

- *Fast oxidative glycolytic* – The cyclist's good friend. They can burn oxygen, so contribute to endurance, but can also contribute to higher power muscle contractions – just what you need on a short hard hill or when trying to catch up with another rider. These fibres can also be trained to act more like slow oxidative fibres.

The percentage of each type of fibre within your muscles – a percentage which you are born with – by and large determines which type of sport or even discipline within a sport that you are likely to be good at. It is generally believed that you can't change the percentage of fibre type within your muscles, but you can increase their efficiency and size – since just like any other physiological system in the body, muscles respond and adapt to training. So, when you commence your cycle training programme, you

7

will begin to improve the strength and efficiency of your muscular system – a very important health-related fitness component. The effects of endurance training on muscle structure and function are shown in Table 1.3.

Generally, cycling tends not to produce sufficient stress to build muscle bulk; rather, it can enhance muscle tone by burning off fat stored between the muscle fibres. Some individuals, however – particularly those new to cycling – will see significant gains in the size of their leg muscles. It is also worth remembering that since cycling will develop mainly lower body strength – being a leg-based exercise – you may also wish to train other muscles (such as those of the arms, back, chest and abdomen) to achieve total body fitness. Some appropriate muscle conditioning exercises are discussed at the end of Chapter 6, pp. 84–91.

Heart rate and training zones

For the 'average' cyclist the most appropriate and accessible way to assess 'fitness level' is the heart rate response to exercise. This is outlined briefly below and in more detail in Chapter 5 on Training Principles .

Oxygen is carried around the body in the blood. It clings to a component of the red blood cells known as haemoglobin in order to travel from the lungs to exercising muscle. The red blood cells carry oxygen first from the lungs to the heart, a muscle which acts as a pump; the left side or ventricle pumps the blood around the body, while the right side returns deoxygenated blood to the lungs to be 're-loaded' with oxygen. The amount of blood ejected from the left ventricle during contraction of the heart muscle is known as *stroke volume* and can be increased through regular aerobic exercse. This is an important health-related benefit resulting from regular aerobic exercise.

When you start to exercise your heart rate increases – in order to pump blood more quickly and meet the greater demand for oxygen of the working muscles. Therefore, changes in your heart rate give an indication of the demands which the exercise is

Table 1.3 *Effects of endurance training on muscle structure and function*

Increase in:
Number and size of mitochondria, the energy production sites within the muscles where aerobic metabolism occurs
Enzyme levels that generate ATP aerobically, without the production of lactic acid
Number of enzymes that facilitate fat metabolism – an alternative route of energy production
Capacity to metabolise glycogen
Size of slow-twitch muscle fibre
Blood capillaries around the muscle fibres – thus increasing the amount of oxygen getting to the mitochondria so that more fuel is available
Amount of myoglobin – the muscles' own internal oxygen store

placing on your cardiovascular system. This in turn provides a measure of how hard you are working: in training terms, of your training intensity. Thus, you can also use your heart rate to establish your individual training zone. The training zone is usually expressed as a percentage of what is known as your *maximum heart rate range*. Both of these concepts are examined in more detail in Chapter 5, pp. 56–7.

Improving cardio-respiratory fitness

Improvements to your cardio-respiratory fitness are directly related to the degree of physical stress which you place on the body through cycling. The three important components of fitness training are:

- *frequency* – or the number of times one trains
- *duration* – or the length of time of any given workout
- *intensity* – simply defined as how hard one is working.

These three components are discussed in more detail in Chapter 5, pp. 54–8. Depending on their interaction within a sustained exercise programme, the maximum amount of oxygen which you can utilise during exercise – known as 'VO_2max' – may increase by up to 30%, especially in individuals with an initial low-level fitness and those who lose a lot of weight[2]. Due to its rhythmic and aerobic nature, cycling is an excellent endurance-based activity for the improvement of VO_2max and therefore of total cardio-respiratory fitness. The effects of endurance training on the cardio-respiratory system are summarised in Table 1.4 – these changes are both the result and cause of increased efficiency in the system, whether it's more blood per beat, larger diameter blood vessels, or more efficient use of fuel by muscles.

Table 1.4 Effects of training on the cardio-respiratory system

Increase in:	Reduction in:
Volume of blood pumped per heart beat (*stroke volume*)	Heart rate at a given intensity
Amount of blood pumped per minute (*cardiac output* = rate × *stroke volume*)	Blood flow neede to the muscle for a set level of exercise (from increased efficiency of ocygen extraction)
Oxygen extraction at the muscle capillary interface	Blood pressure (systolic and diastolic)
Volume of respiration (each breath, tidal volume)	
Breathing frequency with exercise	

[2] Wasserman et al *Principles of Exercise Testing and Interpretation*, 3rd Edition, Philadelphia, Lippincott Williams and Wilkins, 1999.

In summary

It can be seen from the brief outline above that a regular, sustained exercise programme in general, and cycle-specific training in particular, can bring about huge gains in fitness and health – and therefore in what is often referred to as 'quality of life'. The following pages aim to show that even a complete newcomer to the bicycle can quickly and easily take up this highly enjoyable activity and see improvements over a very short time.

Part II
The cycling toolbox

Handlebars

Front brake

Front forks

Dropout eyelets

Quick release axle

Stem

Front derailler

Pedal

Toptube

Crank

Chainset

Saddle

Seatpost

Rear brake

Rear cassette

Rear derailler

Bottom jockey wheel

Figure 2.1 Getting to know your bike

There are four main forms of cycling available to the fitness enthusiast: indoor, road, off-road and track. Your choice will be affected by many factors such as where you live, your budget, the extent of your adventurousness, and the fitness goals that you wish to achieve. This chapter will examine the alternatives in turn, seeing what they have to offer in terms of fitness gains and enjoyment, and also exploring them in terms of financial commitment and possible hazards.

Choosing your cycling activity

Indoor cycling

Whether in the home or at a gym or health club, cycling on an ergometer – an 'exercise bike' – offers the opportunity to gain a good level of aerobic fitness without venturing outside. Many stationary cycles have electronic monitoring which you can use to set and achieve performance goals. Although this is often frowned on by mainstream cyclists, there is no reason why your entire cycling fitness programme cannot be accomplished indoors. Indeed, if you live in a particularly hilly area, a stationary cycle may be a necessary tool for gaining the initial fitness required to conquer the surrounding roads.

Many fitness centres offer 'spinning' sessions, where members of a group ride at the same time while following the directions of an instructor. If you already use the facilities at a fitness club, stationary cycling can provide a stimulus for fitness without many of the costs involved in the more traditional forms of cycling. Having said that, if you confine your riding to stationary cycles, you are missing out on such pleasures as the exhilaration of cycling downhill at speed, or travelling through beautiful countryside under your own power. Below are listed the main advantages and disadvantages of indoor cycling.

Road cycling

This can be recreational or competitive. Recreational cycling foregoes the structure and planning required for serious racing or touring. There is seldom a requirement to purchase specialist lightweight equipment and provided you have a safe and correctly sized bike, regular rides of between 20 and 60 minutes can be both enjoyable and highly beneficial to your fitness.

Riding on roads or on cycle paths is by far the most popular form of cycling. It presents the opportunity to explore your local area and, given a reasonable level of fitness, the novice cyclist can soon be travelling 30–50 km in a training ride. Although increasing traffic volumes pose some safety hazards to the road cyclist,

Table 2.1 Indoor cycling

Advantages	Disadvantages
• relatively cheap • a good opportunity to exercise with others • minimal skill required • some machines offer the facility for upper body exercise • avoids hazards such as busy roads • easy to monitor progress • more easily incorporated into other 'total-body' fitness activities when cycling at a gym • offers more privacy • ideal for those living in hilly or mountainous areas – gives a good base fitness	• high boredom factor may restrict training duration • usually a high-temperature environment • travelling to a gym or health club can be inconvenient • more time in uninterrupted training – with no pauses for junctions, traffic, and so on – means a greater chance of developing cycling ailments such as saddle sores and aching joints

Table 2.2 Road cycling

Advantages	Disadvantages
• readily accessible roads and tracks • little specialist equipment required, therefore cheap • excellent for developing aerobic fitness • cycling speed can be exhilarating • good opportunities for club or social riding • great distances can be covered • enjoyable scenery • emergency help is seldom far away • a cost-effective and pleasurable means of transport	• cycling on congested roads can be hazardous • steep hills may cause initial problems • cycling in a social group requires some skill • poor road surfaces can cause problems in many areas – both rural and urban

even the most congested cities have traffic-free parks, paths and tracks which can be explored. The rural cyclist may have a myriad of small country lanes to explore, and many waterways have adjoining paths which are suitable for cyclists. The speed that can be achieved on a paved road is exhilarating and has led many mature, 'born-again' cyclists back to the freedom of childhood activities. At the outset, even if your ultimate aim is road touring or racing, specialist equipment is seldom required. Many top road-racing cyclists started out by riding their mother's shopping bike!

Table 2.3 Offroad cycling

Advantages	Disadvantages
• high adventure and exhilaration factor – a degree of mud may be part of the equation! • freedom from traffic • a feeling of being closer to nature • good opportunities for club or social riding • development of excellent technical ability (bike control skills) • satisfaction from learning new skills • upper-body fitness also developed • mountain bikes can also be used for road riding • most easily accessible cycle sport for those keen on competition (*see* p. 124)	• a sturdy, purpose-built bike is required • requires more skill than other forms of cycling, depending on the terrain • travel to suitable off-road tracks may be necessary • extreme terrain can be hazardous, especially if cycling alone and a long way from assistance

Off-road cycling

The invention of the mountain bike by American Cycle in the late 1970s has brought to fitness enthusiasts a superb means of improving fitness – with the added challenge of developing the necessary bike control skills for cycling over rough terrain. Despite its name, the mountain bike should not be considered merely as a tool for climbing mountains; most people have nearby access to an area of land suitable for off-road, traffic-free cycling, and in many cities there are dedicated recreational areas for this purpose. Indeed, many people use mountain bikes on the road. It should be emphasised, however, that while mountain bikes can be suitable for most off-road and on-road cycling for fitness, road bikes are not suitable for rough terrain – they lack the requisite durability and manoeuvrability (*see also* pp. 16–23 on choosing a suitable bike for your chosen activity).

Track cycling

Riding on an indoor or outdoor cycle track, or 'velodrome', is seldom a viable option for the fitness enthusiast. The small number of tracks available, the need for specialist equipment and intitial instruction, and the fact that most track sessions are aimed at the competitive cyclist, make the track an environment best suited to the more experienced, conditioned athlete. In addition, track riding requires a bicycle with no gears or brakes and a 'fixed' wheel, which does not allow the rider to stop pedalling at any time – if you are moving, you must pedal. This can be daunting. However, if the thought of racing around a banked oval track appeals to you, there are often sessions designed to teach novices the basics of track riding.

Table 2.3 Track cycling

Advantages	Disadvantages
• excellent means of developing aerobic fitness • excellent means of undertaking high-intensity training • good opportunity for all-year-round competition	• specialist equipment required • good fitness level a prerequisite for most track training sessions • track sessions usually of a competitive nature • high level of skill required • few tracks available • high bordome factor during long training rides

Before embarking on a fitness training programme, consider carefully which of the above options – or what combination of options – will be most suitable for you. The likelihood of successfully starting and maintaining an exercise programme will be greatly influenced by the level of enjoyment which you gain from your chosen activity. 'Severe' mountain bike riding may offer greater potential fitness gains than riding an exercise bike in your home, but this is of no comfort if you are gripped with fear at the thought of riding over rough terrain. Choose your activity carefully and you are much more likely to embark on a fitness programme which will not only enhance your health, but also give you pleasure and enjoyment in the years to come.

Choosing a bike

Having chosen your cycling activity, you may now be faced with the possibly daunting task of selecting the appropriate equipment. There are different bikes available to suit all fashion preferences, rider skills, ages, riding terrain and budgets. However, there is really only one trap which you should be careful not to fall into. Study any cycling magazine and you will see many nice, new, lightweight and probably expensive bicycles. The people riding them will be slim, clean and expensively equipped and clothed. Contrary to the message this conveys, it is *not* necessary for anyone to have expensive cycle equipment in order to undertake an effective fitness programme. What *is* essential is that you have a bicycle which fits you correctly and is in sound mechanical working order, and that you are safely equipped and dressed in comfortable clothing. You may have a bicycle in the back of your garage that your mother used to ride. If it is mechanically sound and fits you well, this bicycle is good enough for fitness training – you will get no fitter riding an expensive new bike straight from the cycle shop. Many riding champions started off on a bike that would be looked down upon by the more 'snooty' cycling aficionados. By all means purchase expensive equipment for the pleasure it may bring, but don't feel that it is essential for fitness training.

When faced with choosing your bike, you will need to decide between one of six main types. The main features of each are described and illustrated below.

Types of bike available

Stationary bike

Also known as an 'exercise bike', or 'cycle ergometer', the correct choice will make the difference between seeing your fitness develop and progress, or having to find room in the attic for another well-intentioned fitness purchase. The best stationary bikes will have a large metal flywheel, which spins smoothly as you pedal. Most now have some form of integrated computer which allows you to monitor your training. It is a good idea to have a look at a local fitness club and see which stationary bikes they use, and then to spend perhaps the first couple of months of your programme using them. This will tell you whether or not you'd prefer outdoor riding. Bear in mind that saddles and pedals may need to be changed to suit you and thus ensure comfortable riding, and be sure to set up your riding position as you would for outdoor riding (*see* also pp. 25–30). A good alternative to the stationary bike is to use a 'turbo-trainer' which simply attaches to your normal bike so you can use it indoors. The picture above shows a typical stationary bike that might be found in your local gym.

Road bike

Road bikes with 'skinny' tyres (18–30 mm) are still popular for racing, long recreational rides, touring, and fitness cycling. The classic racing or competitive riding bike will have larger and much narrower wheels than the mountain bike (*see* p. 20), and a narrow saddle. A racing road bike may be as light as 8 kg, as opposed to 12 kg for the mountain bike. Almost all new road racing bikes are fitted with 16-speed gearing (*see* p. 24).

Sport or Touring bike

This has wide-range gearing, and is a good choice for riders who need some carrying capacity but do not require the very low gears or tough frame and wheels that a mountain bike offers. Its drawbacks are a slower ride and less agile handling compared with the more nimble sport and racing bikes. This is because the frame is designed for stability when carrying heavy loads.

The expedition or old-style touring bike, which is designed to carry 50 pounds of camping gear, will have wider tyres – up to 35 mm – and will weigh more than the sport bike, but will be comfortable for all-day rides. The addition of a third chain-ring will provide low gearing for steep ascents with luggage. Most racing bikes and most sport or touring bikes use traditional 'drop' handlebars the width of the rider's shoulders, although tourers tend to use a wider bar which bends less tightly in the drop section.

Mountain bike

A true mountain bike is more durable than a road bike and can take the abuse of unpaved, unknown trails. It has smaller wheels than a road bike (26 inches or 650 c) and a fatter tyre (up to 100 mm wide) with aggressive tread patterns and a greater capacity for holding air. A flat or curved handlebar and a slightly more upright riding position also distinguish it. Its structure enables it to manoeuvre readily on rough terrain, at both fast and slow speeds.

Mountain bikes are usually 2–3 kilos heavier than equivalently priced road bikes, with a frame size 2–4 inches smaller for a given rider. This again allows greater manoeuvrability and reduces the risk of injury from crash impacts on the top tube. Many mountain bikes are now sold with a front suspension system, usually in the form of telescopic forks. Some designs include rear suspension.

Hybrid bike

The 'hybrid' bike is basically a mountain-style bike that has been optimised to work better on light pavements and trails. It's lighter and rolls more freely than a mountain bike, but is sturdy enough for some trails. Its wheels are of the same diameter (700 c) as a road bike, but the tyre width is narrower than that of a mountain bike. Its upright riding position is also like that of a mountain bike. A hybrid is probably the bike most suited to recreational riding and general fitness training.

Track bike

This is the simplest type of bike, with a racing-style frame and size but no gears or brakes. The rear wheel lacks any free-wheel facility, so that when the bike is moving, the rider has to pedal. If you do choose track cycling as your route to fitness, you would be well advised to contact your nearest track to try out their bikes before making a purchase.

Guidelines to help you choose your bike

In order to decide which of the above types of bike will be most suitable for you, first assess where you want to do most of your riding. Do you want to ride on- or off-road, on a track, along a canal towpath, through a park, or over mountain trails? Then bear the following guidelines in mind:

- An efficient racing or sport-touring bike is best for the open road. As road riding is least punishing on equipment, the old bike in the back of your garage may be perfectly adequate.

- For combining road riding with light off-road (such as towpaths or forest-fire roads), a hybrid is ideal.

- For mostly off-road riding, you'll need a mountain bike.

- For urban commuting, mountain bikes and hybrids are popular, but a road bike will work just as well if you have heavier than normal tyres and wheels to reduce the risk of damage from broken pavements and glass.

- If you intend riding alone, the slower speed of a mountain bike or hybrid may be fine. However, trying to keep pace in a group or with a friend on a road bike when you're on a heavier, slower mountain bike could completely discourage you from social riding.

- High-performance road and mountain bikes often lack facilities for attaching racks, as well as the stable handling required to tote heavy loads. If you are likely to be carrying anything like camping equipment or shopping, buy a bike with 'dropout eyelets' (these are the recesses on a bicycle frame into which the wheel axle is placed – *see* fig. 2.1). Then you can attach racks to mount panniers and other bags, giving you enough capacity for a shopping trip or touring holiday.

Table 2.5 Summary of bike specifications

Component	Type of Bike				
	Road	Sport/Touring	Mountain	Hybrid	Track
Tyre width	18–30 mm	35 mm	up to 100 mm	30–50 mm	18–30 mm
Weight	8 kg	10 kg	12 kg	10–12 kg	8 kg
Gearing	16 speed wide range	wide with ultra-low for touring	very low range	wide range	no gears
Wheel size	700 c	700 c	650 c	700 c	700 c
Handlebar	dropped	dropped	flat	flat	dropped

Making your purchase

Avoid cheap mail-order bikes. They may be suitable for a few years of abuse by a growing child, but their unwieldy weight and inferior quality will soon dampen your enthusiasm. Instead, look in established bike shops, where there are high-quality products and skilled personnel who will help you to select a bike that fits your body and your needs. In addition, they will be able to undertake any maintenance work your bicycle may require.

Although it may be early days in your cycling exploits, try to be realistic about how committed a cyclist you are likely to become. You'll be disappointed at the performance of a budget bike if you aim to ride hard and fast, perhaps with a view to racing one day. An expensive bike designed for the rigours of competition will be wasted on short, casual weekend rides on your local bike path. If you expect cycling to become an increasingly important part of your life, it pays to buy a better bike than your current fitness requires. Then as you progress as a rider, you'll still own a suitable bike.

A good entry-level bike should have a strong but light frame made of steel alloy or aluminium. Preferably, wheels will have aluminium alloy rims (they're actually stronger than steel and make the bike accelerate, handle, and stop better), as well as sealed or shielded bearings to keep the hubs and pedals turning smoothly without the need for frequent maintenance. Brakes should be strong and not fade or 'bite' too suddenly. The gear-changing system should be foolproof with shift levers that have audible click stops. Such 'index shifting' systems, introduced in the 1980s, are now used by cyclists at all levels – they make shifting as easy as tuning a push-button car radio.

A question of gears

Bicycle gears normally consist of different-sized 'cogs', over which the drivechain runs. By moving the chain across the various cogs, the gear ratio is altered. The overall purpose of gearing is to enable the rider to maintain a constant pedalling speed whether climbing, descending, or cycling on the flat.

The usual means of assessing a gear is by measuring the distance (in inches) that the bicycle will travel after one full revolution of the pedal. This can vary from 40 inches to 120 inches (101.6 cm–304.8 cm). For the purpose of cycling for fitness, it is sufficient to know that the lower the gear the easier it is to pedal – and conversely, the higher the gear the harder to pedal.

If you're already fit for cycling, you could probably cope with the higher, more closely spaced gears of a road-racing bike. Higher gearing allows you to ride faster, but requires more force to be generated by the muscles, and therefore a higher level of fitness. If you're not that fit, but your goal is to become so, a racing or sport touring bike is still appropriate if you choose one with a moderate gear range. Alternatively, ask your cycle dealer to substitute a wider-range rear gear set.

If you have no interest in riding hard and fast, and want to pedal as painlessly as possible, the wide range and ultra-low bottom gear of a hybrid, tourer or mountain bike is for you. If you buy a mountain bike, you'll have plenty of low gears; these make pedalling easy in most conditions, and even if you are race fit, you will need them to climb the steep hills typical of off-road riding. The steeper and/or longer the hills that you will face when riding in your local area, the more you'll appreciate a bike with low gears. Do bear in mind though that a cycle shop will be able to change your gears to make steep hills easier should you buy or already own a bike with high gearing.

Fitting your bike

All bicycles used for training and racing should be properly fitted to the rider. A knowledgeable rider can usually fit their own bike; others should go to an established bike shop for advice. Without specialist help, you can assess a frame's suitability by examining the 'crotch clearance'. This is the space between your body and the top tube when you stand flat-footed in front of the saddle. If you know your inside leg measurement, the difference between this and the stand-over height of a bike is the crotch clearance. (Your inside leg can be measured by standing against a wall in your bare feet and placing a pencil between your legs. Move the pencil as high as you can until it rests against your crotch, and then place a mark on the wall. The distance from the floor to the mark is your inside leg measurement.) Traditionally recommended clearances are as follows and are the same for both men and women.

When in doubt about the frame for any type of bike, get a smaller frame; it will be lighter, stiffer, and easier to handle. On bicycles with a sloping top tube, use the 'virtual' stand-over height – that is, where the tube would be if it were horizontal instead of sloping.

The length of the top tube should allow a comfortable riding position with the elbows slightly bent, no matter where one grips the handlebar. The back should flatten when the hands are in the drops. Don't expect the handlebar stem to make up for too much variance in the top tube length, since either a very long or very short handlebar stem can compromise handling.

Table 2.6 Crotch clearances

	Road	Mountain	Touring	Hybrid Road	off-road	Track Racing
crotch clearance cm (inches)	2–2½ (1–2)	7.6 (3)	2½ (1)	2–2½ (1–2)	7.6 (3)	2–2½ (1–2)

Women and 'cycle fit'

Although over 50% of adult bicycle riders are women, most bikes are still designed by, and sized for, men. In relation to their height, women generally have a shorter torso and longer legs than men, so that usually a bike that is built for a man needs a top tube between 1 and 2 cm shorter if it is to be used by a woman.

Traditionally, women's bicycle frames were designed for 'step-through' to assist mounting and dismounting when wearing dresses. This design is still available but is less rigid and strong than others, so that most women cyclists today use a 'man's' frame, suitably adjusted.

Many women are missing out on cycling comfort for want of a few simple adjustments that can bring vast improvement – even though these adjustments are usually small and can be carried out reasonably cost-effectively. There are three main ones, relating to the handlebar stem, the brake levers and the saddle.

- A typical, stock handlebar stem forces women to lean further over the frame than men, putting pressure exactly where it is least wanted – on the front third of the crotch. Ask for a shorter stem to be fitted, so that you can keep your elbows bent when you ride. Remember that although a flat back is recommended for racing, it's not ideal for many women riders because of the likelihood of knee to breast contact – as well as increased pressure on the front of the pelvis (*pubis symphis*).

- Many women experience an ache in their hands after a long ride. It isn't necessary – brake levers with a shorter reach are the answer. They will prevent the need to stretch your hands to apply the brakes.

- If you bought your bike off the floor in an average bike shop, chances are it has a long, thin, flat seat – perfect for men, but completely unsuitable for most women. A saddle is designed to provide support to three areas of bone in the pelvis – one at the front (*pubis symphis*) and two at the rear (*ischial tuberosity*). Because the female pelvis is wider at the rear, saddles are available with a wider rear section. Some also have cutouts at the crucial point of contact with the seat, and can greatly reduce discomfort from pressure and friction.

The more women insist on buying frames of the correct proportions, the more readily manufacturers will respond to their specific requirements. If your dealer is not sympathetic, find another one.

Positioning

It may seem odd that a book on cycling for fitness should devote a lengthy section to the relatively simple concept of correct cycle setup. However, failure to establish a comfortable position on a bicycle will do more to inhibit a successful training programme than most other factors. This section will help you find your optimal riding position. Even experienced cyclists may find that there are points which they have missed, so, while aimed primarily at the novice, this information is important to all cyclists.

Setting up your riding position

There are two common errors that are made by 8 out of 10 novice cyclists. The first is that they have the saddle set too low. This places a great strain on the knees and the thigh muscles and makes swift progress a real burden. The second is that they place their heel, rather than the ball of the foot, on the pedal. Eliminating even these two simple mistakes will greatly enhance a cyclist's efficiency, and is an important first step in correct positioning. When achieved, this will give a feeling of sitting 'within' the machinery of a bicycle, rather than simply being perched on top of it.

Saddle position

Assuming that you are riding a bicycle which is the correct frame size for you (*see* pp. 25–6), the first step is to set the saddle at the correct height. Many adults set their saddle so that when stationary, they can place their foot flat on the ground. Although many of us were taught this as a child, it will not give you an efficient riding position. If you consider the fact that when cycling you are rarely stationary, it does not really make sense to compromise efficiency in favour of comfort when stopping and starting. The guidelines below are aimed at determining a suitable position for most cycling activities. A few cycle sports require more extreme positions, and these can be very efficient; however, for the fitness enthusiast, the following is an ideal starting point for maximising both comfort *and* efficiency.

- Begin by setting the saddle height to allow full leg extension when the heel is placed on the pedal at the bottom of the pedal stroke. So, when you are seated on the saddle with your leg straight, your heel should just reach the pedal (*see* fig. 2.2). When your foot is correctly placed on the pedal – with the ball of the foot above the pedal axle – your leg will be slightly bent at the knee and you will be in an effective cycling position (*see* fig. 2.3).

Figure 2.2 At correct saddle height, you should easily be able to reach the pedal with the heel when the leg is stretched

Figure 2.3 At correct saddle height, your leg should be not quite extended when the ball of the foot is on the pedal at its lowest point

Figure 2.4 A plumb line dropped through the knee should pass through the pedal spindle

• The next stage is to slide the saddle on its rails – either forwards or back – so that the centre of the front knee is directly over the pedal spindle when the cranks are horizontal. This fixes the position of knee, femur and pelvis in proper relation to the bike frame and the cranks (*see* fig. 2.4).

• Holding the saddle level, look at it from the side. The broad area of the saddle – and *only* this area – should be perfectly level when you sit on it. In other words, not the whole saddle. Depending on the particular design of your saddle, it may be necessary to tilt the nose of the saddle up, but no more than 5 degrees. Levelling this broad area prevents you from sliding forwards, planting you firmly on the saddle and cradling you while riding. You may need to re-adjust your seat height slightly to compensate for this angle adjustment (*see* fig. 2.5).

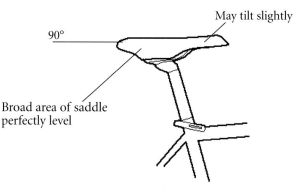

Figure 2.5 Saddle position

Handlebar position

There are differing schools of thought on the height the handlebar should be set. However, for the purposes of fitness cycling you should aim for heightened comfort and control with your back at an angle of approximately 45 degrees while your hands are on the highest part of the handlebar (*see* fig. 2.6). This can be achieved by raising the stem and/or rotating the handlebar until the brake-hoods are slightly more upward. Although your position will be slightly less aerodynamic as a result – possibly making riding into the wind unpleasant – you can remedy this by 'crouching' over the bike (bending your arms at the elbows) when necessary. A more upright position will also help you to breathe more easily because your lungs are not as compressed as they would be if you were leaning over. If your bicycle frame is the wrong size for you, it may not be possible to achieve this position.

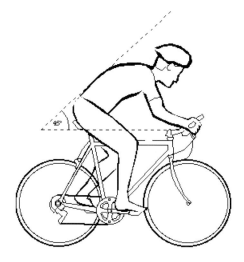

Figure 2.6 Correct cycling position – back at 45° to tube

Positioning your feet

The ball of your foot should rest on the pedal, immediately over the pedal axle (*see* fig. 2.7). The exception to this rule is when mountain biking over rough, 'technical' terrain. In this case having your feet slightly further forward will reduce the stress on your calf muscles. If you are using cycling shoes with cleats attached to the soles, you will need to adjust the cleats so that when you are clipped into the pedal, your foot will be in this more effective, forwards position. It may take some trial and error before you find the perfect setting.

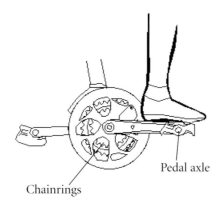

Pedal axle

Chainrings

Figure 2.7 Correct position of foot on pedal

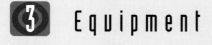

3 Equipment

The advice given in the previous chapter will have helped you choose and fit a suitable bike. However, you still aren't quite ready to ride! There are some items of equipment that you must invest in for your safety and comfort. Others are optional accessories which can make cycling more enjoyable.

Essential equipment

Cycle helmet

It is unfortunate that there are some cyclists who do not regard a helmet as perhaps their most essential purchase. However, many riders who do have walked away from spills that might have resulted in serious head injuries if they had not been wearing a helmet. I have personally destroyed several helmets through hard crashes, yet remain reasonably unscathed! A helmet will protect your head from serious injury in most types of incidents – from impact with an errant driver to an off-road crash onto rocks.

Today, it's easier than ever to protect yourself, because modern helmets are generally light, well ventilated and attractive. Putting one on is as natural as fastening a car's seatbelt. However, you will only get maximum protection from your helmet if it fits well – it is surprising how many riders have never properly fitted their helmets and suffer discomfort ride after ride, while the helmet may not really help when they crash. In normal riding the fitting pads keep your helmet sitting in place, but the straps are critical when you crash and your head is suddenly and violently jerked about. Without them the helmet can come off and leave your head unprotected.

To begin with, make sure your helmet is the right size. They come in many sizes and shapes: egg-shaped, pointy, elongated, narrow or wide. Choose one that is suitable for you; your local cycle dealer should be able to guide you in making the correct purchase. Also check that your choice meets the recommended ANSI and SNELL safety standards.

Figure 3.1 Cycle helmet

Helmets always have at least one set of foam fitting on the inside. Many come with more than one set, and the second – or even third – set of thicker pads can be used to customise the shape. The objective is to make the helmet fit with pads touching your head all the way around, without making it so tight that it will be a constant nuisance.

Put the helmet on and fasten the buckle. Take a few minutes to figure out the strap configuration and keep fiddling until you get it right. Then adjust the length of the chin-strap so that it is comfortably snug. It should be snug against your chin, with the 'V' of the side straps meeting just below your ear. There should be no slack to let the helmet rock back and forth. When you are done, your helmet should feel solid on your head but comfortable. It should be worn horizontally, not tipped back with the front pointing upwards – this exposes your forehead dangerously to potential impact. You will know if you are wearing a helmet correctly – you should forget that you are wearing it most of the time, just like a seatbelt or an old pair of shoes.

Clothing

For general training, padded Lycra shorts, a moisture-wicking undervest, a short-sleeved cycling shirt, and cycling gloves offer a sensible choice. This will allow you to cope with temperatures of between 16°–25°C in relative comfort.

Be sure to match your clothing to the conditions. Nothing can make you more miserable on a long ride than wearing the wrong clothes (except, perhaps, a series of mechanical failures). There is a wide variety of suitable clothing available, so with a little forethought you can be equally comfortable riding in a summer heat-wave or on a cold, wet winter evening. The following are some suggestions for a variety of climatic conditions. Whatever you wear, the visibility of your clothing should be a major consideration; bright, reflective clothing is essential for safety when riding in 'hostile' traffic or, for example, on dimly lit country lanes.

Humid and hot

In humid, hot weather, 'wicking' is the key word, meaning the transportation of moisture away from your skin to the outside environment. Various synthetic fabrics such as 'Coolmax' permit wicking, keeping you dry (or at least drier) and more comfortable.

Hot and dry

In such weather, your sweat evaporates before it gets a chance to perform its cooling duties. A suitable fabric will therefore be a blend that incorporates cotton for a softer, more natural feel and synthetic fibres to enable wicking. You might want to consider bringing an emergency water-resistant layer along, just in case of sudden downpours – or as chill protection in the evening or on a long descent, when you may have worked up a sweat getting to the top.

Cold and dry

Start with a wicking layer, then add layers of insulating synthetic fabrics such as polyester fleece. The number of layers will depend on the extremity of the weather and on your own body temperature. Finish with a wind-proof and water-resistant shell layer. Waterproof fabrics – even 'Gore-tex' – do not breathe as well as most lightweight 'water-resistant' fabrics and may leave you chilled by the accumulated sweat under your jacket.

Wet and cold

No sooner do you hit the trails, then the rain blows in. This kind of rain can feel colder than snow, the wetness seeming to penetrate to the very marrow of your bones. Be prepared. Layer well (*see Cold and dry* above), but instead of finishing with a lightweight, water-resistant fabric, you'll need a shell that is truly waterproof. Be sure that you choose fabrics that are also breathable, otherwise you will create your own rainstorm under your jacket.

Cycle shorts

These are available in touring and racing models. Both types have a large piece of material called a *chamois* (which can be natural or synthetic) sewn into the seat. This provides a smooth, absorbent, padded surface between you and the saddle, which reduces chafing. Cyclists generally don't wear anything underneath such shorts, although if you wish to, seamless underpants can reduce discomfort caused by chafing.

Another advantage of cycle shorts is that they're built to move with you, as opposed to regular shorts that can bunch and bind. Touring and mountain-biking shorts sometimes have pockets on the sides of the legs, rather than at the front, to prevent irritation from items such as keys. Some pockets are zippered or snapped to keep items from falling out.

Racing-style shorts are made of stretchy, body-hugging fabrics such as Lycra. These are generally without pockets, although some have an internal key-holder sewn into the waist. Such shorts should fit snugly without being restrictive. The more contoured fabric panels, the better the fit (eight panels signify premium quality). All shorts are not created equal, and women in particular should be aware that there is now a growing number of clothing companies which cater for their specific needs, offering a more appropriate cut of material and shape of inner padding.

Wash shorts after *every* ride to prevent rashes and sores. Lycra models with a synthetic chamois usually dry overnight, but it's a good idea to have a second pair so that one is always ready for you to wear.

Gloves or mitts

Cycle gloves are an important piece of safety equipment, because in a fall – when your hands naturally go out to protect your body – their thick, padded palms will prevent cuts and bruises. Gloves also distribute the pressure of the handlebar across your palms, thereby preventing blisters, chafing and nerve compression. You can choose from models with foam, gel, or liquid cushioning. A good fit means no looseness or binding, with tight, even seams that won't unravel. Toweling fabric on the thumb or back provides an absorbent surface to wipe your mouth or nose.

Other essential equipment

Tools

A small saddlebag, which attaches underneath the saddle, is an inconspicuous and handy way to store emergency items. However, there is unfortunately no single, correct answer to the question of which tools you should carry on a ride. It may help to ask yourself three questions.

- How well do I maintain my bike? Poor maintenance at home means a specific bike failure is more likely to occur.

- Which repairs am I able to make? Unless riding with another more experienced cyclist, there is little point in carrying tools for repairs that you can't carry out.

- How far from civilisation will I be riding? If you only do day rides close to home, flat-tyre tools and coins for the phone may be enough.

Although each bike may require different tools for maintenance and repairs, most modern bikes are standard to the extent that the following will be sufficient for the majority of on-road repairs and adjustments.

Essential tools

- tyre levers

- spare tube

- hand-pump

- patch kit

- adjustable wrench, 6 mm

- screwdrivers (straight and Phillips head, as appropriate)

- hexagonal (Allen) wrenches of 4, 5, and 6 mm

There are many 'multi-tools' on the market which are specially designed for cyclists and which incorporate many of the necessary tools in one small package, thus cutting down on the carrying space required (*see* fig. 3.2). Before embarking on your training programme, make sure you have all the tools you need and that you understand how to use them. Remember that tools alone won't fix your bike – *you* have to know how to operate them!

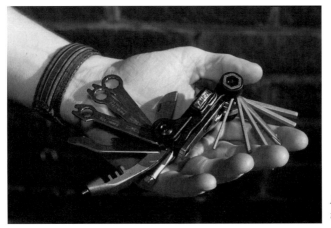

Figure 3.2 A typical multi-tool

Water bottle and cage

These will sometimes be included in the purchase price of your bicycle. If not, buy two of each. Regular intake of small amounts of fluid is essential when riding – not just on hot days, but on cold winter days too.

Lights

These are essential if you plan to ride in the early morning, at dusk, or at night – or, if you suspect that anything may cause your ride to finish after sunset. If most of your training will be carried out in poor light it may be worth investing in a high-powered, re-chargeable system. Such lights are bright enough to allow full-blown mountain biking at night! Otherwise, battery-powered lights can provide more than adequate vision and safety cover. Whichever lights you choose, be aware of the battery run-time and carry spare batteries and bulbs. Always use reflective clothing and accessories to increase the chance of being seen by others.

Bicycle lock

If you intend to park your bike in a public place, you will need to secure it. Choose the most expensive lock you can afford, and ensure that you lock the bicycle to an immovable object! If your wheels have quick-release levers, remove the wheels and pass the lock through the frame and both wheels.

Optional equipment

Cycle shoes

Shoes specifically designed for such activities as tennis, running and aerobics have built-in cushioning for shock absorption. When you wear these shoes for cycling, much of your energy output is absorbed by the cushioning before it ever gets to the pedal. A bike shoe however, has a firm sole, so that more of your pedalling effort actually propels the bike. Instead of flexing, the shoe remains rigid and the majority of the force generated is transferred to the pedal, thus assisting forward movement.

However, while cycle shoes can make you more 'efficient', their stiff soles make walking difficult. Touring shoes offer an acceptable compromise between efficient energy transfer and comfort when walking. Toe-clips go a step further; these consist of a cage attached to the pedal that you slip your foot into and tighten. A clipless pedal system offers the most technological advantage by attaching your foot to the pedal with special pedals and a cleated shoe. Whatever your footwear, avoid riding with the heel of your foot over the pedal. It is much more comfortable and efficient to place the ball of your foot over the pedal axle.

Eyewear

Sports glasses become more popular each year, and with good reason since they offer protection from wind, dust, bugs, grit, glare and ultraviolet light. Look for sports glasses that wrap around the field of vision, permitting a good peripheral view. The lenses should be distortion-free and made of a shatterproof material (the latter is essential for mountain bikers.) A neutral grey, green or blue tint is best for bright daylight, while clear or amber lenses are recommended for cloudy or rainy weather.

Cycle jerseys

Cycle jerseys have several advantages over T-shirts. They're made of fabrics that wick moisture away from the body to speed evaporation. During cool weather this prevents you from feeling cold and clammy, while during warm weather it keeps you from overheating. The stretchy fabrics are cut in panels to match body contours in the cycling position and thus enhance comfort; they are available for both men and women. Jerseys also have pockets in the back where you can stash extra clothing or snacks. Road riders should pick a light, bright colour for maximum visibility in traffic or on evening outings.

Training aids

Getting on your bike and riding as much as you can is really the best way to improve fitnesss. However, some training aids are available which can help you to work more efficiently – as well as allowing you to train when it would otherwise be impossible. Nearly all the cycle magazines advertise a great deal of merchandise which the manufacturers claim will make you a better rider. In reality, there are really only two proven aids to the cyclist in serious training: the *heart rate monitor* and the *cycle computer*. Knowing how hard, how far, how fast and how long your training has been can be a great help in controlling and monitoring your progress, as well as adding interest to your rides and maintaining your motivation.

Cycle computers

Cycle computers are mostly small, flat multi-functional instruments which attach to the handlebar (or, when integrated with a heart monitor, are worn on the wrist) and provide feedback on your performance in a variety of ways. A typical computer is shown in fig. 3.3. They work via magnets attached to the wheel spokes and a sensor attached to the fork blade or chainstay. The computer is set for the diameter of the wheel. Each time it senses the magnet passing, it performs the necessary calculations for a readout on the display. Calculates can be metric or imperial, and use a 12-hour or 24-hour clock. Most are accurate to within 0.5 mph and change readings each second. Function results are usually rounded to the nearest tenth or hundredth of a second.

Figure 3.3 Cycle computer

Many cycle computers display more than one function at a time and offer a choice of screens and displays. When making a purchase, it is a good idea to hold the screen away from you at approximately 'handlebar' distance to make sure you can read the display. Not all of them have the same functions, and there is no sense in paying for something you don't need and won't use. Below are listed some of the main features available; after a short time in the saddle, you will know which ones will be helpful to you.

Main features of cycle computers

- *Auto start or stop.* This is useful if you only want to know your average speed or trip time when actually moving.

- *Average speed.* This is calculated via the trip odometer (*see* below) and the clock. Some average speed functions will automatically shut down when the bike is stationary.

- *Trip distance.* The distance travelled since starting your ride.

- *Cadence.* This is your pedalling speed, in revolutions per minute.

- *Clock.* To tell the time.

- *Heart rate.* A sensor is worn on the chest and transmits to the computer without a wire (*see* p. 38). Pulses are timed by the clock and expressed as beats per minute. Target heart rate zones can be inputted, with a 'limit alarm' set to sound when the user goes above or below the desired heart rate – or cadence, speed, and so on.

- *Maximum speed.* The computer continually compares your current speed with the highest speed previously recorded on the same trip, and saves the highest speed reached into the memory. In some computers, this feature retains the highest speed attained since the batteries were fitted.

- *Odometer.* This records the distance that the bike has travelled. It records the cumulative distance registered until the battery is replaced or a maximum number is reached, at which time it re-sets to zero.

Heart rate monitors

The heart rate monitor uses a chest strap with an inbuilt sensor to detect the electrical activity of the heart muscle (*see* fig. 3.4, p. 38). It then transmits this information to the wristwatch receiver, where it appears in beats per minute (*see* fig. 3.5, p. 38). The rate at which your heart beats is a good indicator of the amount of oxygen that your whole body is processing. There are certain levels of oxygen consumption which, if maintained, will bring about beneficial gains in performance (*see* pp. 9–10). While there is no machine to tell you what your oxygen consumption is while training, you can use a heart rate monitor to give you a good indication and adjust your programme accordingly.

Heart rate monitors can be purchased from £55 upwards, at the time of writing. The basic models are of use to any fitness enthusiast; the more expensive memory models are really only appropriate for dedicated racing cyclists.

Recently a new breed of heart rate monitor has become available which can record such data as speed, distance, average speed and time, in addition to heart rates. In other words, it combines the functions of a heart rate monitor and a cycle computer. Obviously, an ability to download such a variety of data from training rides and races enables you to monitor and analyse your performance in detail. In addition, some advanced models look for variations in the time gap between each heartbeat. This gives an indication of the responses of the nervous system – a possible indicator of the athlete's state of fatigue. With the correct interpretation of data, training sessions can be adjusted to make them highly specific to race situations and minimise the time spent at less effective training intensities.

Figure 3.4 Chest strap

Figure 3.5 Heart rate monitor

Part III
Training for fitness

When undertaking a training programme, it is important to have a good grasp of the necessary safety precautions and technical considerations that will make it as risk-free and effective as possible. This chapter examines the key issues of bicycle maintenance, basic riding technique, and on- and off-road safety. Depending upon your chosen activity, it may not all apply to you; but for the sake of your and other people's welfare, it is a good idea to make sure you are aware of the content.

Bicycle maintenance

When you go for a bike ride your body will get a workout, and so will your bike. Have you checked your bike for mechanical safety? Timely bicycle maintenance can prevent a serious accident. Here is series of checks which you should carry out every time you ride.

Your wheels

Check the tyre pressure. Tyres should be inflated to the rated pressure noted on the sidewall (pounds per square inch, or bar). Use a gauge to verify that you have reached the recommended rate – if you don't have a floor pump with a gauge, use the finger tests, as follows:

- A road bike tyre should be inflated until it won't deform when you try to press your thumb into the tread.

- A mountain bike tyre should deform by 3–4 mm when you try to press your thumb into the tread.

Check for damage to the tyre sidewalls and the tread. Sidewall damage is common if the brakes aren't adjusted properly. If the bands of the tyre are showing below the surface, you need a new tyre.

Your quick releases

These are the means of attaching the wheels to the frame. Quick-release hubs need to be tight, but not too tight. The proper pressure is obtained by pushing on the quick-release lever so it leaves an impression on the palm of your hand. The closed lever should face up and back to minimise the chance of catching on anything while you ride. Quick-release brakes, which are opened when removing or installing wheels, need to be in the closed position. When closed, check to make sure the brake pads aren't rubbing the rims.

Your brakes

Visually check the brake-block pad for wear. If less than 2 mm of rubber shows at any place, have the brake-block or pad assembly replaced. Make sure that the brake blocks are almost parallel and aligned with the side of the rim when applied (the front area of the pad should contact the rim first by 1 mm). Check the cables and housing. Cables need to travel smoothly. If they stick, apply lubrication at the ends of the housing and work it in by applying the brakes several times. Frayed cables should be replaced.

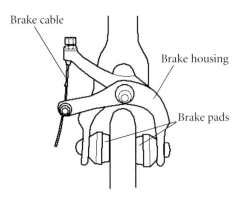

Figure 4.1 Brakes

Your drivetrain

Check the crank set. This consists of the bottom bracket, the crank arms, and the chainrings. To do this, take the left and right crank arms in your hands and attempt to move them sideways. If both move, you have a problem with the bottom bracket. If only one moves, the individual crank arm is loose and must be secured. A loose crank arm should never be ridden.

Finish your pre-ride checks with a brief, slow ride to check that your gear derailleurs and shift levers are working properly. If you find that your bike needs adjustments beyond your ability, enlist the mechanics at your local bike shop – don't risk riding it until faults have been successfully remedied.

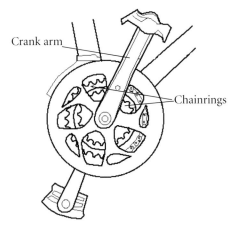

Figure 4.2 Front of drivetrain

Basic riding technique

Starting and stopping

Instead of using both feet to push off the ground to gather speed, put your weight on one foot and position the other pedal at the two o'clock position. Most people discover that there is one leg they prefer to use to start pedalling. When you wish to start riding, push down on this pedal and you'll have enough momentum to balance and begin pedalling. If you use toe-clips or cleats, wait until you are safely through a junction or onto a road before you clip in with both feet.

When stopping, remember that you don't have brake lights, so make your intentions known to other road users. Apply your brakes and as you slow to a standstill, remove your left foot from the pedal and place it on the pavement. Alternatively, slide forward off the saddle and lower an unclipped foot to the ground.

Correct pedalling

It is generally taught that pedalling should be about pulling as well as pushing. In reality, even top professional riders are producing negative force on the up-stroke. In other words, they aren't moving the foot up fast enough to get out of the way of the pedal – which is being pushed up by the combined force of the down-stroke and downward momentum on the other side. Try to get your feet out of the way as quickly as possible; this will help to improve the speed and efficiency of your pedalling.

You should aim to pedal at a constant speed all the time – ideally, between 70 and 90 pedal revolutions per minute. The novice may need to build up to this gradually. Persevere, and you will be a much smoother, more efficient cyclist as a result. As the route steepens or descends, use changes of gear to maintain this pedal speed – a lower gear on hills, a higher gear on descents. So, at 8 mph or 28 mph your pedalling speed should be the same, with your choice of gear determining the speed at which you're travelling. In this way your cycling will be most effective and you will experience optimal fitness gains.

Relax and keep comfortable

Efficiency on the bike is influenced by how relaxed and comfortable you are whilst riding. Assuming that you're riding a properly sized and adjusted bike, maintain your comfort by changing hand position often, keeping your elbows relaxed, and gently stretching out your neck and shoulder throughout your session. Stretching is discussed in detail in Chapter 7.

On- and off-road safety

Safe riding in traffic

Knowing how to handle the various traffic situations in reasonable safety and with reasonable efficiency is essential. Fear of traffic has been shown by many surveys to discourage a large number of would-be cyclists from taking up the activity. However, since the traffic conditions generally regarded as most frightening are frequently those that are easily handled by reasonably competent cyclists, it is reasonable to conclude that learning basic traffic skills removes one impediment to cycling as a fitness, recreational and sports activity.

Positioning on the road

Traffic laws in the United Kingdom direct cyclists to ride 'as far to the left as is possible'. (Reverse this and the following advice for countries where you drive on the right.) So exactly how far left is that? It doesn't mean you have to ride in the gutter and dodge drain grates, glass and gravel. It does mean you need to ride far enough to the left to allow traffic to pass, if it's safe for you to do so. And it is up to *you* to decide whether or not it's safe.

(a) Wide road   (b) Narrow road

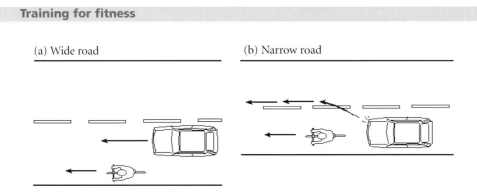

Figure 4.3 Desired positioning when cycling on the road

Because bicycles are narrow vehicles, it is often possible to share a traffic lane with another vehicle, as illustrated in fig. 4.3(a). However, if the lane is too narrow for you to share safely, ride far enough to the right to fully occupy the lane. Where the left-side wheel of cars would be is a good spot, most often free from debris which could cause a puncture. This position is shown in fig. 4.3(b). Overtaking motorists will not be able to squeeze past you while remaining in the lane, so they will have to acknowledge that they are passing another vehicle, wait for oncoming traffic to clear, and pull across the central line. Overtaking cyclists could still share the lane, so don't assume that you own the lane while riding in this blocking position. Always look behind you before moving left or right within the lane.

In a very wide lane there might be room for you to ride several feet from the curb and still allow room for traffic to pass to your right. There are no good reasons to move left in this situation, and several reasons why you are safer away from the curb. You're more visible; there is more time to react to someone opening a car door or pulling out of a driveway; you're not holding up traffic; and there is less rubbish on the road which could cause a puncture. If there are parked cars or other barriers that form a 'wall' near the left edge of the road, move to the right. Give yourself some room to manoeuvre and time to react to conditions like a sudden gust of wind or the impatient motorist who tries to squeeze past you in the lane.

If you are moving as fast as other traffic, move right into the lane. You won't hold anyone up since you are travelling as fast as they are, and you need extra space around you at higher speeds. If you are grinding up a hill at little more than walking pace, move left. At slow speeds it is possible to ride safely within a few inches of the edge of the pavement, though you should always be watchful for glass and other debris.

At road junctions your position in the lane can be a very effective indication for other drivers as to which way you are going. If you are going straight or turning right, move to the centre or right-hand side of the lane. Drivers behind you who want to turn left can then pull up to your left and make the turn without crossing your path as shown in fig. 4.3(c). If you are turning left, keep left, await your turn and when it is safe to do so – as shown in fig. 4.3(d).

(c) Road junctions
turning right

(d) Road junctions
turning left

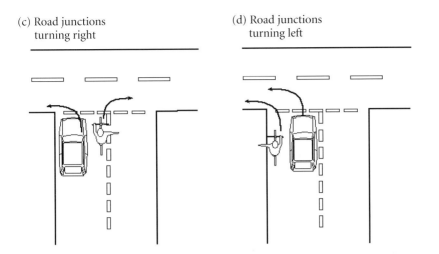

Figure 4.3 (c) and (d) Desired positioning at road junctions

Finally, always follow the rules of the road. Stop for stop signs. Be predictable. There is nothing more delightful than the look of astonishment on the face of a motorist when a cyclist correctly yields to them. Let's be our own best advertisement for our right to share the road.

Avoiding collisions
Riding safely in traffic doesn't have to be a hit-or-miss situation. There are preventative measures which can be taken to reduce the likelihood of a crash, and avoidance techniques which can be employed if a crash is imminent.

Coping with descents
When riding on- or off-road you must be in control of your speed. This requires continuous attention and concentration. Inevitably, you will be faced with a steep descent at some stage, and it is important that you are aware of safe riding practices in such situations. Always pay attention to the route rather than the scenery. Just around the next corner there may be potholes, gravel, a parked car jutting into the road, sharp curves, water on the road, pedestrians, or other cyclists or cars. Maintaining a speed that you are comfortable with will enable you to avoid these dangers.

Long descents may require frequent braking, so apply firm, uniform pressure to the front and rear brakes. Once you have reduced your speed, release them. Constant application of the brakes will overheat the rims and may cause a tyre to burst. If your bike begins to wobble during a fast descent, stay calm. The geometry of some bike frames and forks (wheels out of true or loose components) may cause your bike to shake at high speeds. If this occurs, continue to apply your brakes intermittently until you have slowed down – the wobble should subside at a lower speed. When you have come to a complete stop you can check your bike for mechanical problems.

> **Training tip**
>
> It is tempting to freewheel on descents, but continuing to pedal when riding downhill serves an important training function. It aids the removal of waste products from the muscles, and the return of de-oxygenated blood to the heart.

Descending around corners

As you approach a corner, slow down when you're still travelling upright in a straight line, so you don't have to brake as you are leaning over. Apply more braking force to the front brake as long as you are upright and travelling in a straight line. Braking during a curve may cause skidding and loss of control of the bike. Ride with your body in an upright position in the saddle. This will create additional air resistance and will help to slow your speed. Keep both hands on the handlebar.

Remember to remain in the same relative portion of the lane when riding a curvy descent. When a corner is so tight that it requires you to stop pedalling and freewheel, straighten your outside leg, pedal down, and apply some pressure on this outside pedal – this will enhance your grip and stability in the corner. Be very aware of the centrifugal forces on tight curves, which will send you away from the apex of the corner.

Figure 4.4 Cornering on a descent

Riding in the rain

Wet roads require heightened attention to the above techniques. You must control your speed even more. Roads are slippery when wet, and your brakes are much less effective. At times you may need to keep a constant, light pressure on the brakes to sweep the water off the rims so you'll have some braking power. If you do get caught in the rain, always use extreme caution.

Dealing with dogs

Dogs love cyclists – that is, they love chasing them! Providing advice on how to deal with dogs in every situation is impossible. Different dogs, like their owners, have different personalities; and opinion differs too on how to cope with troublesome dogs – some advocate the aggressive approach, others the passive. Many dogs will retreat if you employ the time-honoured technique of shouting 'No!' or 'Home!' These specific words are often familiar enough to startle the dog and cause it to stop dead in its tracks. Other 'scare' tactics include pretending to throw something or spraying the dog in the face with drink from your water bottle. More drastic measures like kicking out are not recommended because you will be forced to sacrifice control of your bike. Some people promote talking to the dog in a calm voice, since many dogs are more interested in chasing a cyclist than in biting one. It is better not to take a chance by coming to a complete stop to scratch the dog behind the ears; you never know how it might react.

No matter what method you choose when dealing with a dog, you need to avoid hitting it with your front wheel. If your wheel is diverted, the end result is likely to be a fall; and while most people worry more about being bitten, dogs tend to cause injuries to cyclists much more frequently by causing falls. If and when you come upon that 'mad dog', keep both feet on the pedals, both hands on the handlebars, and be ready to apply the brakes. Only after your front wheel is past the dog should you worry about being bitten.

Mountain bike skills

If you have chosen to use a mountain bike to gain or improve personal fitness, and you intend to venture off-road onto rough terrain, you are sure to gain immense pleasure from your cycling. However, there will undoubtedly be obstacles along the way which must be overcome – indeed, it is these very obstacles which make off-roading as challenging and enjoyable as it is! Like any activity requiring skill, it will take time to learn the most effective techniques, but there are some guidelines which will help you from the start. Most importantly, look where you want to go. Your bike follows your head. Scan the track ahead, letting your eyes rove from 15 m, to 10 m, to 5 m and then to 2 m in front of you before looking ahead again. Know what's coming and pick your line accordingly. Don't look at the things you don't want to crash into, because you will find yourself deviating towards them. Bear in mind that there are only two kinds of mountain biker: those who have fallen off their bikes, and those who are going to fall off their bikes. As long as you expect a few tumbles, you won't be too upset when they happen!

Riding over obstacles

If you're out on the trail, sooner or later you're going to have to ride over something; perhaps a 4–5 inch high obstacle such as a rock, branch or ledge. The great thing about a mountain bike is that it's designed to get over obstacles easily. You, as pilot just need to remember some helpful pointers.

- You will often need *speed* to get over things, otherwise an obstacle will stop you dead when you hit it and you risk falling. Remember to keep your speed up until you are only a couple of feet away from the obstacle. If heading uphill, you're going to need to keep pedalling until you clear the obstacle, and then keep pedalling afterwards.

Figure 4.5(a) Absorbing the obstacle

Figure 4.5(b) Moving your weight forwards

Figure 4.5(c) Rear wheel over

- Many mountain bikes are fitted with front and sometimes rear suspension, but *your body is the biggest and best shock-absorber.* Use it to your advantage. Loosen up. Make sure your knees, elbows, shoulders and wrists are ready to flow.

- *As you approach the obstacle*, transfer your weight through your legs onto your pedals (make sure these are level with one another). Keep your hands off the brakes. Use the handlebars to steer you directly perpendicular to the obstacle. Move your bottom slightly up off the seat. Move back slightly.

- *When you reach the obstacle*, shift your weight to the rear of the bike and keep a solid grip on the handlebars. Keep the front wheel straight at all costs. When the front wheel hits, absorb the impact by bending your elbows and knees. Don't fight it. Think about 'sucking in' and absorbing the obstacle in order to stay stable. The front wheel will rise towards your body: let it come. This is shown in fig. 4.5(a).

- *After your front wheel makes it over*, straighten your arms by pushing the handlebars away from you. Don't lock your elbows, just move them to a straighter angle. This helps move your weight forwards on to the front tyre again (*see* fig. 4.5(b)). Now stay off the saddle, and let the rear wheel roll over the obstacle (*see* fig. 4.5(c)). The bike's over, you're over. Scan the trail ahead, put your rear back on the seat, stay loose, and enjoy the ride.

Climbing hills

Figure 4.6 Correct position for climbing steep hills

Don't ride up hills, ride *over* hills. Inexperienced cyclists faced with hills tend to shift into lower gears as they progress higher, gradually slowing down and fading completely at the top. Most experienced riders who ride over hills shift into bigger gears as they go, gradually speeding up near the top, and maintaining this speed after the hill stops. The key is to pace yourself from the bottom of the hill. Remember that the ride doesn't finish at the top of the climb, and ride *over* lots and lots of hills and *up* none!

Never avoid hills when riding. They are the key to both aerobic conditioning (*see* p. 70) and developing muscle strength and endurance. If you don't like riding uphill, it's a sure sign that you need to ride uphill!

Climbing hills requires a little preparation, but the key is to get comfortable. Your position, the gear which you select and the speed at which you travel will affect your ability to reach the top in one piece. You need to look ahead, take stock of the hill, and try and judge a few key things.

- What front chain-ring should you be in, given your strength and the steepness of the hill? If it's really steep and long, shift down into the smallest chain-ring. If it's medium, maybe the middle one. Your left hand controls this.

- It's important to shift into the chain-ring you want to climb in *before* you start uphill, otherwise you can run into problems. If you need to, work your way down the smaller gears as you climb.

- As you shift, make sure you're pedalling smoothly. Do not stop pedalling, shift the gear, then start pedalling again – you should aim to shift without putting climbing pressure on the chain. Also, try not to change the big chain-ring as you climb. If you do need to go down to a lower gear, make sure it's a smooth transition, without pressure on the chain.

Overall, you want to be pedalling smoothly and efficiently. It should be hard work, but not impossible. Stay seated if you can. Keep your weight over your rear tyre; this gives you better traction. If you find your front wheel wobbling or coming up, move forwards on the seat a bit, but keep your weight on the rear tyre. And initially, don't be ashamed to get off and walk if the going gets too tough!

Starting on a steep hill

After stopping or falling from your bike, you need to get started again. If you're going uphill, and it's fairly steep, what should you do?

- Find a comfortable starting spot. If you can find flatter terrain, great. If not, go for it or push.

- Start in the right gear. This is one that gives you forward momentum when you start. Too low and you'll spin the wheels, lose momentum, and fall; too high and you won't be able to pedal at all.

- Straddle the bike, hands on the handlebars, with both brakes locked. Put one foot on your pedal or in your clip, usually your stronger leg. Your pedal should be in the two o'clock position. Keep your other foot on the ground.

- With everything in place, pull the handlebars back towards you, push off with your grounded foot, and push down hard onto the pedal with the other. Bring your other foot up on to the other pedal and keep pedalling. Don't clip into your pedal until you've gained traction and maintained your balance. Stay over your seat to keep the traction.

- When both your feet are in and you're moving along comfortably, sit back down on the saddle and ride onwards and upward.

Steep descents

The exhilaration you can gain from riding a mountain bike downhill at speed is the reward for the effort required to reach the top of the hill! On normal descents the same rules apply as for road descents (*see* pp. 45-6). However, when things get really steep you need some different techniques.

- Move your body weight further back. In some cases, you may need to slide all the way off the back of the saddle – practise this skill.

Figure 4.7 Correct position for steep descents

- Stop pedalling. Keep your pedals horizontal to avoid catching your lower foot on anything, and ensure that your weight is on the balls of your feet and stabilised through your thigh muscles. Do not lock your knees – your legs are the ultimate shock-absorber. Extend your arms (almost fully) in a nice relaxed position. Do not lock them.

- Try to steer by shifting your hips and bodyweight rather than the wheel. If you do use the wheel, turn it very slowly and smoothly.

- To brake, use the rear and 'pump' the front. Be careful not to lock the brakes, especially the front.

- Finally, start slowly. There is no need to go fast until you really start to master the required skills.

The off-road code

There are several well-established rules that all mountain bikers should learn.

- *Ride on legally open trails only.* You must not ride on public footpaths.

- *Don't leave evidence of your passing.* Do not ride under conditions where you'll leave evidence of your passing, for example, on certain soils after a rain storm. Practise low-impact cycling. This also means staying on existing tracks and not creating new ones.

- *Ride in control.* Control is the key to fun riding.

- *Yield the trail to other users.* This includes both walkers and horses. Make your approach well known in advance. A friendly greeting or bell is considerate and works well; don't startle others. Anticipate other trail-users around corners or in blind spots.

- *Never scare animals.* Most animals are startled by an unannounced approach, a sudden movement, or a loud noise. Give animals extra room and time to adjust to you. When passing horses, use special care and follow directions from the riders (ask if uncertain). Worrying cattle and disturbing wildlife are serious offenses.

- *Leave gates as you find them* – or as marked.

- *Plan ahead.* Make sure you have all the equipment you need. Nothing ruins a great ride like a long, long walk. Be self-sufficient at all times, keep your equipment in good repair, and carry necessary supplies for changes in weather or other conditions. Always wear a helmet when riding off-road, and ride with a friend.

The fact that you are reading this book means that you have decided that your fitness is important. It is likely, too, that you are considering cycling as your chosen path to enhanced fitness and health. However, 'cycling' is a broad term; it covers a wide range of activities, each exerting different demands upon the body. The businessman who rides an exercise bike in the privacy of his bedroom is just as much a cyclist as the young mountain biker hurtling down an alpine trail.

Before looking specifically at *Cycling for Fitness*, it is important to consider the basic principles behind the commencement of any exercise programme. In order to build fitness training into your lifestyle, and to benefit fully from its effects, you have got to make a commitment – to have real 'staying-power'. However, it is also important to decide quite early on what level of fitness you want to achieve. Fitness is very personal – what is 'fit' for your friend may not necessarily be 'fit' for you. Though you may be restricted by such factors as age and genetics, you can greatly improve the quality of your life by initiating and maintaining a balanced exercise routine, and at the same time improving your nutrition (*see* pp. 105–118). Rome was not built in a day, and – although you will feel the benefits of your training quite quickly – getting fit will take some time, too. It is important to persevere!

Before going any further down your chosen route to fitness, you should first establish that your basic health is able to withstand an increase in your level of physical activity.

Checking your health

It is generally accepted that vigorous exercise involves minimal health risks for persons in good health or those under medical supervision. Far greater risks are presented by habitual inactivity and obesity. As a rule, if you are under 35 and in good health, you probably do not need to see a doctor before beginning an exercise programme. However, if you are over 35 – and especially if you have been inactive for several years – you should consult your physician, who may or may not recommend a graded exercise test. There are certain conditions in particular that indicate a need for medical supervision or clearance.

Conditions requiring medical clearance

- high blood pressure
- heart trouble
- dizzy spells
- breathlessness after mild exertion
- arthritis or other bone and joint disorders.

If you know that you suffer from any of these conditions or you are pregnant, you are already likely to be under medical supervision. Otherwise, you can gain some indication by carrying out a quick self-check. Start by answering the questions below.

- Has your doctor ever said that you have a heart condition and that you should only do physical activity as recommended by a doctor?
- Do you feel pain in your chest when you do physical activity?
- In the past month, have you had chest pain when you were *not* doing physical activity?
- Do you lose your balance because of dizziness or do you ever lose consciousness?
- Do you have a bone or joint problem that could be made worse by a change in your physical activity?
- Is your doctor currently prescribing drugs for your blood pressure or heart condition?
- Do you know of any other reason why you should not do physical activity?
- Are you pregnant?
- Do you suffer from diabetes?
- Do you suffer from epilepsy?

If you answered 'Yes' to one or more of the above questions, it is very important that you talk to your doctor before you start a training programme – or increase the intensity of an existing one. Remember, the above is only designed to give you an indication; if in any doubt, consult your doctor.

Some general principles of training

As discussed briefly in Chapter 1, 'training' in simple terms involves subjecting your body to 'stress' – both psychological and physical – and then allowing it to adapt so that it will be able to cope with similar stress in the future. If we make the stress specific to the demands of cycling, the adaptations will enable us to ride further and faster than would previously have been possible.

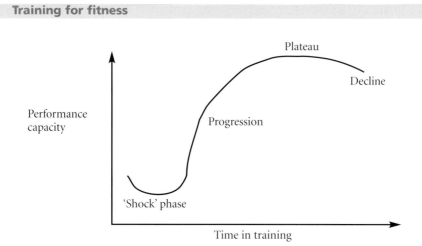

Figure 5.1 The law of diminishing returns

When you start training, your body goes through an initial 'shock' period during which it struggles to adapt to the stress of training. For example, you may experience a day of muscle pain following your first fast, hilly ride. Soon, however, you will start to see significant gains – perhaps making a marked improvement in the time taken to ride a particular route. In time, the rate of this progression slows; and after a period of dedicated training it is quite common to arrive at a 'plateau' in your fitness – and in many cases, a decline. This is known as the law of diminishing returns, and is illustrated in fig. 5.1.

When planning a training programme there are many rules or 'principles' which must be applied if optimal results are to be gained. Failure to adhere to any one of these will prevent you from making the most of your training time. Six of these principles, which explain how and why training works, are explored below. Chapter 6 examines how you can manipulate your rides to achieve your fitness goals – in effect, the practical application of training theory.

The overload principle

If you ride over the same distance at the same speed for every workout, there will be no continued improvement beyond the point to which your body has already adapted. In order to gain fitness from any training activity, you must exercise against a resistance greater than that which is normally encountered. This process is known as *overloading* the body. Such an overload results in fatigue, followed by recovery, and eventually a greater degree of fitness (known as 'overcompensation' – *see* p. 58 below). Many riders fail to load or 'stress' their body sufficiently after initial fitness gains, and as a consequence, fail to see improvements in their performance. If your training has been the same for the past few years then you need to introduce some additional overload. (This is known as 'progression' – *see also* p. 58 below.) You can do this in three different ways – separately or in combination – each of which is examined below.

1. Intensity of training

This may be simply defined as how hard you are training. In order to plan an effective training programme based on overload and progression, it is necessary to have some means by which you can assess the intensity of your riding. There are many ways in which intensity can be quantified, however, only three are of practical use to the cyclist.

- Speed
- Subjective feeling – perceived exertion
- Heart rate

Speed
The first is actual speed – how fast you are travelling, or how quickly you cover a set distance. A cycle computer can give you this information (*see also* pp. 36–7). However, while these are within the budget of the majority of riders – and offer many useful functions – they cannot by themselves give you the required data for setting your training intensity. The reason for this is that your body has no concept of miles per hour; it only knows how hard it is working. For example, you might decide to train today at 17 miles per hour on your favourite route. There's a head-wind, so you're working extra hard to maintain your target speed. Next week there's a tail-wind, so 17 mph is relatively easy. Your heart rate will be faster for the first session than for the second – in other words, your speed is irrelevant as an indicator of your training intensity. If on the other hand you decided to train at a *heart rate* of 150 for an hour, the conditions would be irrelevant – your speed would vary, but your body would be working at a set level and that's what matters.

The one instance when speed can be a useful indicator is if you track your average speed over the same route as your fitness programme progresses. Provided the ride is done under similar conditions, on the same equipment, you will have a rough guideline as to your progress.

Subjective feelings – perceived exertion
Subjective feelings, or rating of perceived exertion (RPE), can be an excellent means of assessing training intensity. Using an RPE scale, you rate the effort numerically as follows.

Rating of perceived exertion

6	13 – somewhat hard
7 – very, very light	14
8	15 – hard
9 – very light	16
10	17 – very hard
11 – fairly light	18
12	19 – very, very hard
	20

Note aim at 'somewhat hard' – 'hard' (80% maximum)

Heart rate

When you exercise, the rate at which your body consumes oxygen is closely reflected in the rate at which your heart is beating – your *heart rate* (HR). Over recent years, the availability of relatively inexpensive heart rate monitors (*see* p. 38) has had an enormous impact on the fitness industry, enabling athletes in many sports to set training intensity with more accuracy than ever. A monitor is worth getting if you're serious about fitness, but it needs to be used intelligently if you're to see a real gain in the effectiveness of your training.

It is possible to monitor your heart rate quite effectively using a manual method. For this you'll need a watch or a stopwatch and a couple of fingers. First, stop riding – this is advisable, even if you are an experienced cyclist. Then, find the pulse on your wrist with two fingers (don't use your thumb). Count the number of times it throbs in 15 seconds and multiply that by four. This gives you the number of beats per minute. With practice you can do this as you ride, but stopping to take heart rates is better as long as you don't pause for more than 10 seconds beforehand. The figure you get tells you how hard you are working immediately before you stopped; you can then ride harder or easier, depending on the training effect you want to achieve from that session.

Some of the sample training sessions included in Chapters 6 and 9 use percentages of what is known as your *maximum heart rate range* to set the required work intensity. You can work this out as follows.

1.   Find your *resting heart rate*. This is best done when you wake up in the morning and are still lying down, or last thing at night when relaxed. Over a few days you will establish an average resting heart rate.

Resting heart rate = eg. 50

2.   Find your *maximum heart rate*; to do this you can either get a 'guesstimate' by subtracting your age from 220 (which is far from accurate), or work out an actual maximum. Do this by riding gently for 10 minutes, then starting to ride harder and harder. After 5 minutes of progressive riding, sprint uphill as hard as you can for 20 seconds. The heart rate you get should be a maximum.*

Maximum heart rate = eg. 200

3.   Subtract your resting heart rate from your maximum – this gives your *heart rate range*, or how many beats per minute your heart rate can change from its minimum to its maximum.

Maximum – Resting = Range
(200 – 50 = 150)

Do not do this if you suffer from heart problems; if you have been inactive for a year, or you are over 35; if you know of any reason why maximal exercise could be damaging to your health; or if your doctor has ever told you that you should not exercise maximally. If any of these conditions apply to you, get clearance from your doctor before you start to exercise at these intensities.

4. Take the percentage of the range at which you want to train (*see* p. 56). For 60% you would multiply the range by 0.60; for 85% you would multiply it by 0.85.

$$\textbf{Range} \times \textbf{Percentage} =$$
$$\textbf{(150} \times \textbf{0.60} = \textbf{90 (A))}$$

5. Finally, add your resting heart rate (*see* point 1 above) to the number you end up with in (A).

$$\textbf{Resting} + \textbf{(A)} =$$
$$\textbf{(50} + \textbf{90} = \textbf{140)}$$

This will give you your target heart rate.

It may seem complicated initially, but you will find that you can work it out with relative ease. As a general rule, sustained lower-intensity training – which gives you basic aerobic and muscle conditioning, and improves the body's ability to metabolise fat – occurs within a range of approximately 60–75% of your maximum heart rate. For the purposes of optimising your own training, you will need to establish your own resting and maximum heart rate. You can use the guidelines set out in Chapter 6, pp. 66–71 to determine your own individualised heart rate training zones. This can be done manually or by using a heart rate monitor if such a thing is within your budget.

Low-intensity training can be further sub-divided into three phases:

- *active recovery*, at less than 60% of your heart rate training range – this is really training to assist recovery, since light activity is generally considered better for recovery than no activity at all;

- *long slow distance*, at approximately 60–75% of your heart rate training range – most of your mileage work will consist of this, especially when riding to gain base endurance, or 'training to train' (*see also* pp. 69–70);

- *'up-tempo' training*, at approximately 75–85% of your heart rate training range – this bridges the gap between low and high intensity training. Since training intensity higher than these three levels improves the body's ability to cope with acceleration, top speed and speed endurance, sprint recovery, and high exertion levels, it is more appropriately discussed in relation to training for competition, dealt with in Chapter 9 on 'Cycle Sport Training'.

It is these three, lower intensity phases which will contribute to the bulk of any cycle training programme where the main objective is to improve overall fitness and health. According to the American College of Sports Medicine, low- to moderate-intensity programmes with a longer training duration are recommended for most individuals, with a training intensity set between 60 and 80% of maximum heart rate.

Following the advice given above, you can use your heart rate to set your desired training intensity and apply an appropriate overload.

2. Duration of training

This is defined as the length of time you are spending at a given intensity, either continuously or via repeated efforts (known as 'repetitions' – *see* also p. 61). For minimum effectiveness, you need to ride for at least 20–30 minutes within your established training zone. If you feel that this is beyond your current ability, don't worry; start with a riding time which you are happy with and over time you will progress.

3. Frequency of training

This is simply how often you are training. Research indicates that maximum aerobic conditioning occurs as a result of three workout days per week. It is interesting that these three days per week will maximise aerobic conditioning equally in any combination – i.e. three days in a row with four days off; alternating days; and so on. Provided that rides are carried out at an intensity equal to the training intensity that developed the level of fitness in the first place, duration and frequency can be reduced. For example, 12 hours a week at a training level of 75% heart rate range could be reduced to 4 hours per week, as long as intensity is held at 75%.

The overcompensation principle

The process of 'stressing' the body – or a particular system or structure within the body – and then allowing it to recover from that stress is basically a means by which the body survives changes in its environment. After a training session, or series of sessions, your body experiences fatigue. As it recovers, it will undergo a process of adaptation to the training stress which will leave it in a better 'biological state' or condition than before. This is known as *positive adaption*. If then left to its own devices, the body will return to its previous condition. This series of reactions to training stress is known as *overcompensation*, and is illustrated in fig. 5.2.

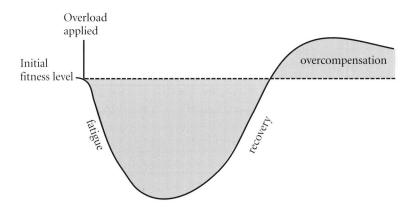

Figure 5.2 Overcompensation

The progression principle

As your fitness improves – as your body adapts to the stress imposed upon it – rides that were a struggle three months ago may now be insufficient to elicit a training response. You must therefore progressively increase the training load; if you don't, you will arrive at a 'plateau' and your performance will cease to improve – or it may even decline (*see* pp. 53–4 on the law of diminishing returns). The *progression principle* dictates that you increase your workload gradually, with periods of rest and recovery prior to each increase. For examples of how to progress your training effectively, *see* Chapter 6, pp. 63–79.

The specificity principle

The muscles that are stressed during cycle training will adapt in highly specific ways to the demands imposed upon them in training. This also applies to other tissues (ligaments, tendons and so on) as well as to physiological systems. If your training objectives include becoming a more explosive sprinter, then you have to train explosively. If you desire greater endurance you must incorporate numerous aerobic capacity rides in your programme. This is the *specificity principle*.

The specificity principle is so 'uncompromising' in its workings that problems frequently arise if a rider is trying simultaneously to achieve gains in more than one area of fitness. The specific training required for one body part or system will frequently detract from the extent to which you can expect to gain in another. For example, training specifically to improve aerobic capacity will severely limit the level of muscular power you can attain. A track sprinter may be at an elite level because of their sprinting power, but they will never match the endurance of a road racer.

The rest principle

Training is a cyclical process of 'tearing down' and 'building up'. The adaptations that we are trying to stimulate via this process require the synthesis of new biological material – and this takes time! Our red blood cells are dying out at the rate of 2–3 million every second, and being replaced just as fast; muscle cells, on the other hand, have a much longer life but are constantly repairing themselves from within. During training intentional, specific damage is done to some cells and cellular resources such as fuel, water and salts are used up. When you finally climb off your bike after a workout, you have not in fact become stronger – you are actually weaker than before you started! How much weaker depends on the severity of the training session. Getting fitter is a process that actually occurs during recovery periods rather than training periods.

Recovery allows the body to repair microscopic damage to muscles, to restore energy levels, and to adapt to the stress of training and racing. It therefore enables better performances in the future. Recent studies on elite endurance athletes have shown marked improvements following up to two weeks of rest. So, bear in mind that repeated training sessions with no time for recuperation will lead to a breakdown, not an enhancement, of your physical condition. This is known as 'overtraining'.

The 'use it or lose it' principle

If you stress your body and its systems enough, it will adapt to meet the stress. If you stop stressing it, it will adapt to meet the decreased stress. In other words, if you stop training, your hard-won fitness will not last forever. Unfortunately, it takes much less time to become 'detrained' than it does to become trained. The good news is that cutting your training volume by two-thirds, but keeping the intensities at the same level, will maintain your condition at close to 100% – this is useful for periods when time or other constraints prevent you from training as frequently as usual.

Summary

In summary, effective training is based on the following stages and inherent principles.

- The 'alarm stage' – application of workload or 'stress', and subsequent fatigue (the *overload* principle comprising intensity, duration and frequency).

- The 'resistance stage' – adaptation of the body in order to cope with the workload more efficiently (the principles of o*vercompensation, specifity, rest* and '*use it or lose it*'). Allows recovery to the overcompensated condition.

The next training session or series of sessions is introduced when you are in an overcompensated state. If you fail to increase the training volume in a progressive manner, the stress will be insufficient to elicit a training response, or you will notice a steady decline in your physical state – the 'exhaustion' stage. You will then be forced to stop riding altogether.

The various methods of training

The training principles discussed above can be practically applied in a variety of ways. Optimal aerobic training, the most important for nearly all forms of cycling, must include a combination of the following types of exercise: *continuous* training, *interval* training and *fartlek* training.

Continuous training

Continuous training refers to aerobic activity performed at approximately 60 to 80% of your maximum heart rate range (levels 9 to 13 on the RPE scale) for at least 20 minutes (*see* p. 57). This level of work is the cornerstone of all endurance training. It is ideal for those starting off an exercise programme; for the elite rider wishing to improve their endurance; for those wishing to maximise calorific expenditure for weight loss purposes; and as an option for an active 'rest' day in a weekly endurance training programme. It may come as some surprise, but the novice who spends 45 minutes riding along at a comfortable level is training in much the same way as a professional cyclist on a 100-mile ride – carrying out continuous, sustained activity, at well below maximal intensity.

At lower levels – around 50% of maximum heart rate range – continuous training is effective at increasing a cyclist's fat-burning ability. This is useful for those aiming for long day tours and distance challenges. However, although these lower levels of training intensity will make one more efficient at burning fat, those riders wishing expressly to lose excess body fat are advised to achieve greater calorific expenditure through more vigorous training levels. Ultimately, the key to fat loss is calorific balance, not the amount of fat burnt during the activity (*see* Chapter 9 on nutrition).

Interval training

This training method involves 'sandwiching' periods of intense physical activity between periods of recovery. It thus enables longer periods of training at high intensity. For example, let's say that it takes you 60 minutes to ride 20 miles. To improve this figure, you could do six 10-minute rides at 22 mph, with a recovery period between each effort. In total you would have covered 22 miles at target intensity, even though the total training distance covered may be more. Adaptation comes from the 22 miles, so that eventually, by gradually reducing the recovery, you will reach the point of being able to cover 22 miles within an hour. It has been demonstrated with runners that continuous, maximal performance levels could be sustained for only 0.8 miles before exhaustion occurred, while a similar level of peak exertion could be maintained for a cumulative distance (duration) of over 4 miles when intervals were used.

Interval training sessions consist of repetitions – often referred to as 'reps' – recovery periods, and sets. A set is a group of repetitions. So, a session could be described as:

- 3 sets of 5 × 1 minute @ 90% max, with 90 seconds recovery – 4 minutes between sets

In this session, the rider would do five one-minute efforts at 90% of their maximum. After each repetition they would recover for 90 seconds before doing the next one. After five repetitions (one set) they would recover for 4 minutes, before completing two more sets.

It is often assumed that interval training should be left to the more experienced athlete. However, after a suitable period – between four and eight weeks – of continuous training, the novice cyclist can improve their fitness considerably by incorporating a basic interval training session into their exercise programme. The interval session described in Chapter 6 (*see* pp. 70–1) is suitable for the novice cyclist, with the needs of more experienced or ambitious riders being catered for in Chapter 9. It is important always to bear in mind that interval sessions are very hard work and so should be used sparingly – they have been known to discourage many a fitness enthusiast when over-used. Don't use them all year round and never more than twice a week. Separate each interval session by at least 48 hours to allow adequate recovery. Figure 5.3 shows the heart rate recording from an interval training session. From this, you can see how the heart rate rises during the work interval and drops again during the recovery phase.

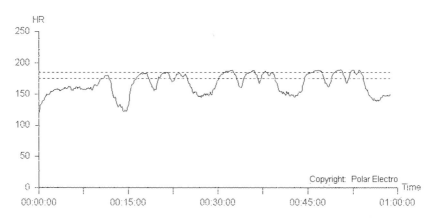

Figure 5.3 Heart rate recording from interval training session

There are some general 'rules' which you should try to follow when doing an interval training session. Many riders think that interval training just means riding as fast as possible, then resting, then doing it again. Close – but not quite. Don't ride as fast as you can, otherwise you'll only be able to manage a couple of attempts before getting too tired to continue. Keep the intensity at a level that allows you to do at least five intervals. Nine repetitions at close to maximum intensity are more beneficial than three reps at max. When resting, you should ride around in a low gear to promote recovery. This is much more effective than just stopping dead, though that's what you may want to do. You should stop a session when you 'lose your form', i.e. when your head droops, your shoulders go wobbly and you have to keep getting out of the saddle to get the gears turning. If you keep going when you're exhausted, you are only training yourself to be slow.

Fartlek training

This form of training originated in Sweden, and translates as 'speed-play'. Essentially, it is a combination of continuous and interval training, with the rider varying work intensity throughout a session as and when they desire. This adds a feeling of freedom to those long, slow days. How many sprints, and for how long? The choice is up to you, but the intervals are probably similar to those used in interval training as discussed above. Adaptation to this kind of training is very specific, so it is more appropriate to advanced training for competition than simply riding for fitness.

6 Planning your training programme

Goal-setting

It is difficult – if not impossible – to plan an effective training programme without first establishing what you want to achieve. If you don't know where you're supposed to be going it's pretty hard to arrive there, no matter how fast you travel. As an integral part of your planning, therefore, you need to set yourself targets or *goals* to aim for.

At its simplest level, the process of goal-setting allows you to choose what you want to end up with at the end of a period of training. By knowing what you want to achieve, you know what you have to concentrate on and improve, and what is merely a distraction. Goal-setting gives you long-term vision and short-term motivation. If you set sharp, clearly defined goals, you can see progress in what might previously have seemed a long and pointless grind. By effectively setting goals you can almost certainly improve performance by improving the quality of your training, increasing your motivation to achieve greater results and improving your self-confidence in coping with challenging training situations.

Research has shown that people who use goal-setting effectively:

- suffer less from stress and anxiety

- concentrate better

- show more self-confidence

- perform better

- are happier with their performance.

Provided that you have the self-discipline to carry it through, goal-setting is also relatively easy. The first step is to decide your level of commitment to your activity. If you want to use cycling as a means to improve your level of fitness, then you will have different goals from someone who has decided to dedicate their life to achieving excellence in cycle sports. Once you have established this, write down a list of your more specific targets. You may find the following guidelines useful.

Guidelines for setting training goals

- Your goals should be positive, rather than an attempt 'not to do something wrong'.

- Be precise. If you set a precise goal, putting in dates, times and other details so that achievement can be measured, then you know both the target and when you have achieved it.

- Don't just have 'being fitter' as a goal. Avoid vagueness. For example, you may decide that you want to be able to cycle comfortably for one hour at the end of three months' training.

- Set out your goals in order of priority. Where you have several goals, give each a priority; otherwise, you can become overwhelmed.

- Keep your immediate goals (i.e. those pertaining to a particular training session) small and achievable. If a goal is too ambitious, then it can seem as if you are not making progress towards it.

- It is extremely important that you set goals over which you have as much control as possible. There is nothing as depressing as failing to achieve a personal goal for reasons beyond your control such as poor judging, bad weather, injury, better competitors, or just plain bad luck. Goals based on outcomes are extremely vulnerable to things beyond your control. Base them on things that *you* can achieve.

- Set specific, measurable goals. If you achieve all the conditions of a measurable goal, then you can be confident and comfortable in its achievement. If you consistently fail to meet a measurable goal, then you can adjust it or analyse the reason for failure and take appropriate action to improve skills.

Setting goals at the right level

It is obvious that your targets need to be realistic, but how can you set goals at the correct level? You should set them so that they are slightly out of range of your current ability, but not so high that there is no hope of achieving them; no-one will put serious effort into achieving a goal that they believe is unrealistic. Take personal factors into account, such as tiredness, injury, work and family commitments, forthcoming races, and so on. Then, when you've set your goals, it's time to go out and try and reach them!

After achieving your goals?

The final aspect of goal-setting is what to do when you've achieved your target. First of all, enjoy the satisfaction of having done it. Be proud; if there is no pleasure in reaching a target, why bother setting new ones? If the goal was a significant one, or one that you had worked towards for some time, a reward may be appropriate. You may want some new cycle equipment – perhaps you should wait until you've lost 5 kilos?

Where you have achieved a goal, this should feed back into your next ones. If the goal was easily achieved, make your next goals harder. If the goal took a depressingly long time to achieve, make the next target a little easier. If you learned something that indicates the need to revise the targets you still have outstanding, then do so. If while achieving the goal you still noticed some deficit in your armory, set goals to fix this. Remember too that goals change as you change. Adjust them regularly to reflect changes in your fitness, skill, or even level of enthusiasm. If goals do not hold any attraction any longer then let them go – goal-setting for performance should be your servant, not your master.

Finally, to motivate any budding world champions, consider this true story – one of the most inspiring examples of goal-setting. In 1972, a student watched the swimmer Mark Spitz win six Olympic gold medals. The student was also a swimmer and decided that he would win a gold medal in the 1976 Games. He worked out by how much he would have to improve his current time in order to achieve this, and his task seemed daunting if not impossible. Then he worked out how much training he could reasonably expect to do in four years, breaking it down into months, weeks, days and hours. The result was that he reckoned he would have to be faster by the blink of an eye for every length of the pool he swam over the next four years. This seemed more feasible. He won three gold medals in the 1976 Olympic Games.

Planning your training

The warm-up and cool-down

When planning any training programme, you must build in as a matter of course two key considerations: a thorough, effective warm-up before, and cool-down after, each and every session. These are a vital part of both preparation and ongoing performance. The general principles are discussed here, with stretching and massage being covered in depth in the following chapter.

The warm-up

For many reasons, the warm-up is a vital part of any exercise programme:

- warming up lubricates your joints by stimulating the fluid that allows smooth movement of bone over bone – the 'synovial fluid'

- lubricated joints help you to move better and that prepares your body for the intense movement of exercise

- warming-up increases your heart rate, so that your heart pumps more blood and takes in more oxygen

- if you start exercising without warming up you risk injuries

- warming up has a psychological benefit, allowing you to focus your mind on your training.

An ideal warm-up would consist of 10–12 minutes of easy to moderate riding, followed by stretching of the muscles in the lower back, legs, neck and shoulders – see Chapter 7, pp. 95–104. A further 5 minutes of riding – with the heart rate being gradually raised to the target levels of the training session – would finish off the warm-up. A warm-up is important even in hot weather – increasing the core temperature of muscles requires activity. Ensure that you have developed a light sweat and slightly laboured breathing before training harder in the heat.

If you are going to undertake an intensive interval training session, you should aim in your warm-up to raise your heart rate gradually to levels close to those anticipated in the main workout. This can be achieved after a continuous, sustained ride of between 10 and 15 minutes at around 65% maximum. After this period, introduce some 10-second maximal efforts, with 50 seconds recovery between each one. After five to six sprints, you should be ready to start the main interval session, well warmed-up and ready for action.

The cool-down
The cool-down is the recovery phase – the point at which you start to recover from the workout you have just finished. It is almost guaranteed that if you do not cool down and stretch after a strenuous workout, you could be in a lot of pain for the next day or two. This is because while training, your muscles are at a higher temperature than normal, receiving a large volume of blood pumped from the heart. However, blood returning to the heart laden with carbon dioxide and waste products is not pumped by the heart but instead relies on muscle movement to 'squeeze' it through one-way valves in the veins. When you stop exercising, the 'venous return' is compromised. This can lead to a delay in the recovery and repair of the muscles.

Once you have lowered your heart rate through gentle riding, you should aim to stretch all your muscles – paying special attention to the muscles you've just worked. Each cool-down stretch should last between 8 and 15 seconds and you should hold the stretch a little longer and repeat it if the muscle feels particularly stiff or sore. Don't overdo the stretching; simply stretch until you feel some mild tension in the muscle. Remember: stretching shouldn't hurt. We will examine cycling specific stretches in more detail in Chapter 7.

Creating a training schedule
Creating a *training schedule* is an excellent way to organise your cycling. With a well-thought-out schedule, you'll have a better sense of where you're headed and how you're going to get there. A good programme should also motivate you. Following your day-to-day progress is enjoyable and encouraging with specific rides to look forward to and, in time, your schedule will become more than an organisational tool – it becomes a challenge and a reward in itself.

The trick is to put together the right schedule. If you set your sights too high, you'll soon get frustrated. If you aim too low, you won't be using your schedule as it can and should be used: to motivate. Don't get locked into the specific elements of your schedule – let them evolve. If you have a ride scheduled one weekend but something comes up, don't worry about it. You want a schedule that's specific enough to keep you interested, but not so specific that you get bogged down in the details. Finally, maintaining a schedule shouldn't be so involved and time-consuming that you quickly tire of it. When in doubt, simplify and stick to the basics. The steps listed below will help you to create the right plan for you.

Identify your base fitness level

The guidelines given on pp. 68–9 will enable you to establish your base fitness level, and to pitch your training schedule appropriately (*see* also pp. 71–6, 'Sample training programmes').

Set your fitness goals

As we have seen above, goal-setting is a key element in both creating and maintaining an effective training schedule.

Identify your training opportunities

Consider how much time you have to train each week (*see also Planning your programme*, below). Be honest, and don't forget to include the time that it takes to get ready for a ride and to change and shower afterwards. Bear in mind your work and family commitments, and factors such as availability of equipment. Finally, take into account *when* you will exercise during the day. The hour just before the evening meal is a popular time for exercise, providing a welcome change of pace at the end of the workday and helping to dissolve the day's worries and tensions. Another popular time to work out is early morning, before the workday begins. Advocates of the early start say it makes them more alert and energetic. Whenever you do decide to exercise, it's important to schedule your workouts for a time when there is little chance that you will have to cancel or interrupt them because of other demands on your time. If you train after work, it is worth having a mid-afternoon snack two or three hours before training to ensure that your energy levels are sufficient. You should not exercise strenuously during extreme hot, humid weather or within two hours after eating. Heat and digestion both make heavy demands on the circulatory system and, in combination with exercise, can be an overtaxing 'double load'.

Identify obstacles in your way

What factor will make it hard for you to undertake or maintain a training programme? Lack of equipment, lack of time, lack of support, or adverse weather? Although you should be aware of these, there are always ways around any obstacle. Some brainstorming and lateral thinking should eliminate obstacles to the point where starting a fitness programme is feasible. It won't always be easy, but if you have truly made a commitment, you will find a way. (*See also* pp. 77–9 below on 'Problem-solving').

Plan your programme – general consideration

If a novice cyclist can find time for 3 × 30 minute sessions each week, they can improve their fitness through cycling. More than that is a bonus – 30 minutes each day would be excellent, and an hour each day fantastic. But start slowly: if you are new to training, 3 × 30 minutes is a good starting point.

As a general rule, train by gradually increasing the duration of rides, then the intensity, then combining the two, then recovering. This works out nicely as a three-week build-up period, followed by a one-week recovery period. The following gives a sample four-week progression at a basic level.

Table 6.1 Sample 4-week training progression

Week	Progression
Week 1	Ride further than you normally do
Week 2	Ride over your normal distance, but at a higher intensity
Week 3	Ride the distances you covered in Week 1, at the intensity of Week 2
Week 4	Ride half the distance of Week 3, at the intensity of Week 2

How often, how long and how hard you exercise within a schedule should be determined both by what you are trying to accomplish – your goals – and by your present fitness level. Look at the following four broad fitness levels, and decide which most closely fits your own. Then, follow the relevant general guidelines to help you build up your weekly schedule. (*Note*: The ride durations given do *not* include the warm-up or cool-down.)

Fitness level 1
You never (or rarely) participate in aerobic activity.
At this level, most experts in the field recommend beginning with three sessions per week, 20–30 minutes per session. If you cannot ride for 20 minutes to begin with, don't worry, just keep at it until you do reach the 20–minute mark. (In order for your heart to benefit, you should try to exercise aerobically for a minimum of 20 minutes – not including warm-up or cool-down.) The key is to begin slowly and gradually work up to more exercise. People who jump from doing nothing right into exercising five or six times a week will burn out and probably injure themselves in the process. If you are using an exercise bike indoors, boredom and discomfort will be the main enemies of an effective programme. The first time you train, see how long you can go before you get fed up with it. Then for your actual programme, just aim to do 80% of this time. This way, you know that you won't get bored each time you start a fitness session.

Fitness level 2
You comfortably participate in aerobic activity for at least 20 minutes three times per week.
Try to increase the duration of your rides to 30 minutes and try to exercise four times a week (rather than three). If you've been doing 20 minutes of exercise, try increasing the duration in small increments (i.e. 22 minutes, then 24 minutes, etc.), rather than increasing the duration by the full 10 minutes – this will make the transition easier.

Fitness level 3
You can ride comfortably for at least 30 minutes, 3–4 times per week.
To increase your level of fitness, try to exercise for 30 minutes 4–5 times per week. (If you are currently at three times per week, increase to four. If you are at four times per

week, increase to five.) Build progression into your plan. You could ride the same distance as usual but try and do it faster, or ride further in the same time. Any of these methods will help to maintain a positive physical stress on your body.

Fitness level 4
You are a regular recreational cyclist who can ride comfortably for more than one hour, more than four times per week.

At this level, your most appropriate means of increasing fitness is to undertake a programme that is based on training for competition. Although you may have no desire to actually race your bike, by following the guidelines in Chapter 9, you will see significant gains in your cycle fitness. The competitive approach will introduce new training stresses, which will elicit greater gains than could be achieved by simply continuing your recreational-style fitness training.

Each and every workout should begin with a warm-up and end with a cool-down (*see* pp. 65–6). Never be tempted to skip them! Finally, as a general rule, space your workouts throughout the week and avoid consecutive days of hard exercise.

Types of training session

In order to understand the principles behind the sample training programmes given in the following pages, it is necessary to look in a little more detail at the three essential ingredients of fast recreational riding: base endurance, aerobic conditioning and aerobic power. Improvements in these three fitness components will permit the enjoyment of hours in the saddle, and potential progression to higher training levels as discussed in Chapter 8.

Training to improve base endurance

Endurance, simply put, is the ability to persist in exercise – to resist fatigue. Building a solid 'base' of endurance fitness comes from time in the saddle and is best gained through long, steady rides away from major climbs.

Base endurance takes a while to develop – around 100 hours of riding for the complete newcomer to cycling. However, just like the foundations of a building, it provides an essential framework to support efficient and effective heart, lungs and muscles. In building base endurance, you are in effect getting fit before you start to train.

Keep your endurance rides low in intensity and do them for as long as you can manage. If you're starting from scratch, 20–30 minutes, three times a week is plenty to begin with (*see also* Table 6.2, p. 72). Such rides have two major benefits:

- They increase fitness without the pain and discomfort that accompanies high intensity riding.

- They teach muscles to burn fat. While fat provides more energy per gram than other fuels, it needs a greater amount of oxygen to burn each gram. At higher intensities, muscle cells cannot process enough oxygen to enable fat to be the main fuel. (For more information on 'fuel for fitness', *see* Chapter 8.)

On endurance rides, the pace should be kept steady and the effort feel comfortable, with a heart rate of below 60–65% max (*see also* p. 57). By taking the time to build such a base, you will progress much faster when the time comes to increase riding intensity – in effect, you'll reach your own potential a lot quicker.

Training to improve aerobic conditioning

This is the next step in your quest for fitness – after the 'skeleton' of base fitness comes the 'meat' of aerobic conditioning (sometimes known as *aerobic development*). The intensity of rides can be increased now, the primary aim being a general improvement in heart and muscle efficiency. Given time, chambers in your heart can actually increase in volume, meaning that more oxygen-rich blood is pumped to the muscles each time your heart beats. In addition, your muscles become more efficient in their use of oxygen and fuel, and more able to deal with the waste products of muscle activity.

To gain aerobic condition you'll need to start to work or 'stress' the heart. This means bringing the riding intensity up from base fitness levels of around 60–65% max, to closer to 75–80% max – equivalent to a moderate to high training load, as shown in the sample training patterns on pp. 72–5. The best means of raising your heart rate on a bike is simply to head for the hills: hill riding is discussed in detail on pp. 49–50. Otherwise, ride hard periodically over mixed terrain – such as rolling roads combined with hills and flats. Just enjoy the feeling! Anything that will raise your heart rate – preferably for at least 10 minutes – before you settle the pace down again will have substantial benefits.

When you have accumulated around 40 hours of riding to improve aerobic conditioning, you will be ready to introduce sessions specifically designed to develop *aerobic power*.

Training to improve aerobic power (VO$_2$max)

Also known as *aerobic capacity* or 'VO$_2$max', this element of fitness may be defined as the maximal capacity for oxygen consumption by the body, during maximal exertion – or, more simply, as maximum oxygen uptake. Aerobic power training sessions are designed to create a stimulus for the improvement of the heart's ability to deliver oxygen to active muscle. Such sessions can help develop speed when done on the flat, or climbing power when the efforts are made over hilly terrain.

Interval training (*see also* pp. 61–2) is one of the most efficient ways in which to develop aerobic power. This is because when your heart beats, a certain volume of blood (which is carrying oxygen to the muscle) is pumped from the left lower chamber of the heart – the left ventricle. The amount of blood pumped per heartbeat is called *stroke volume*. The greatest stimulus for placing stress on your stroke volume – and thus enabling adaptation – occurs immediately after a short, very high-intensity period of exercise. Therefore, intensive bursts of riding will encourage greater adaptation; and building in a recovery period between these efforts will allow you to do a greater number of intensive bursts.

As a result of your training to improve base endurance and aerobic conditioning (as discussed above), you should now be able to ride very hard for 30 seconds. For your aerobic power session, warm up for 15 minutes by doing a ride at about 65% max. Then do your 30-second hard effort – and it should feel hard. Then ride easily for 30 seconds, then hard again, and so on. After five efforts – also known as 'repetitions' – you can have a much longer rest, say 5 minutes of gentle riding. Try to do a further two sets of 5 × 30 seconds, with a 30-second recovery between efforts and five minutes between sets. An interval session such as this will create the stimulus for beneficial adaptations in the heart no fewer than 15 times in just 25 minutes of riding!

Two such sessions each week – and that should be the maximum that you attempt – will enable you to ride further and faster than ever before. To see additional fitness gains, you may need to follow the race training advice given in Chapter 9.

Specific planning

Sample training patterns

When planning your schedule, you need first to decide how to divide the overall training load. Figures 6.l–6.4 give some sample training 'patterns', each of which is linked to the four different fitness levels identified on pp. 66–7. Once you have established which level most closely relates to you, refer to the relevant training pattern.

It is important to bear in mind that these sample training patterns are intended only as a general guide. Don't consider them as strict rules to be followed implicitly – you'll need to change your routine over time in order to allow both sufficient overload, and the necessary recuperation, for a progressive increase in fitness. For example, a rider at level four may well use the first pattern as a recovery week; the rider at level two may attempt level four as a challenge.

Sample training programmes

Optimal training requires a delicate balance of work, or 'stress', and rest. Likewise, the body needs to stay in balance throughout each weekly or monthly cycle of training. As a result, it is important to employ a weekly training schedule that keeps your body well rested while ensuring that progress is made.

Obviously, your own commitments in respect of work, social life, recreation and family will strongly shape your individual programme. Therefore, just as with the training patterns given in figs 6.1–6.4, the following training programmes are intended as an *aid* to planning. They should be used in conjunction with your personal circumstances – thus enabling you to work out a training programme to suit *you*.

Sample training programme for fitness level 1

The training progresses from three 20-minute rides each week, to the addition of hilly routes, longer rides, and longer hilly rides, with the 8-week period leading to an increase in riding time from 60 to 140 minutes per week. You will see that there is no recovery week. At this point in a rider's development, the adaptations to training can occur rapidly and after an initial period of adjustment, full recovery often occurs after a full day's rest. The addition of an extra ride in week four places additional demands on the rider; but as the subsequent sessions are after a day of rest, and are either short hilly or easy rides, there should be no problem adapting.

Table 6.2 Sample 8-week programme – fitness level 1

	Mon	Tue	Wed	Thur	Fri	Sat	Sun
Week 1		Easy 20 min. ride on flat route		Easy 20 min. ride on flat route			Easy 20 min. ride on flat route
Week 2		Easy 20 min. ride on flat route		Easy 30 min. ride on flat route			Easy 20 min. ride on flat route
Week 3		Easy 30 min. ride on flat route		Easy 20 min. ride on flat route			Easy 30 min. ride on flat route
Week 4		Easy 30 min. ride on flat route		20 min. ride on hilly route		Easy 20 min. ride on flat route	Easy 30 min. ride on flat route
Week 5		20 min. ride on hilly route		Easy 30 min. ride on flat route		20 min. ride on hilly route	Easy 30 min. ride on flat route
Week 6		Easy 30 min. ride on flat route		Easy 45 min. ride on flat route		20 min. ride on hilly route	Easy 45 min. ride on flat route
Week 7		Easy 45 min. ride on flat route		20 min. ride on hilly route		Easy 30 min. ride on flat route	Easy 45 min. ride on flat route
Week 8		Easy 30 min. ride on flat route		40 min. ride on hilly route		Easy 30 min. ride on flat route	40 min. ride on hilly route

Sample training programme for fitness level 2

The training progresses from 20-minute rides each week, to the addition of hilly routes, longer rides, and longer hilly rides, with the 8-week period leading to an increase in riding time to three hours per week. The training progression is not always reliant on riding harder and harder. You will see that week 8 contains no hilly or hard rides, the training load coming from the duration of the rides, totalling three hours.

Table 6.3 Sample 8-week programme – fitness level 2

	Mon	Tue	Wed	Thur	Fri	Sat	Sun
Week 1		Hilly 30 min. ride		Easy 20 min. ride on flat route	Hilly 30 min. ride		Easy 45 min. ride on flat route
Week 2		Hilly 30 min. ride	Easy 20 min. ride on flat route	Hilly 30 min. ride			Easy 45 min. ride on flat route
Week 3		Easy 45 min. ride on flat route	Easy 20 min. ride on flat route	Easy 45 min. ride on flat route			Easy 45 min. ride on flat route
Week 4		Hilly 30 min. ride	Easy 30 min. ride on flat route	Hilly 30 min. ride			Easy 60 min. ride on flat route
Week 5		Hilly 30 min. ride	Easy 30 min. ride on flat route	Hilly 30 min. ride			Easy 60 min. ride on flat route
Week 6		Easy 45 min. ride on flat route		Easy 45 min. ride on flat route			Easy 60 min. ride on flat route
Week 7		Easy 45 min. ride on flat route	Easy 30 min. ride on flat route	Easy 45 min. ride on flat route		Hilly 30 min. ride	Easy 45 min. ride on flat route
Week 8		Easy 30 min. ride on flat route	Easy 60 min. ride on flat route	Easy 30 min. ride on flat route			Easy 60 min. ride on flat route

Sample training programme for fitness level 3

This plan leads the rider through two distinct phases of training: weeks 1–3 and weeks 5–7. Weeks 4 and 8 are recovery weeks. The first phase develops fitness through intensity with combinations of hard rides. The second period from week 5 uses an increase in the duration of easy rides as the main source of training progression.

Table 6.4 Sample 8-week programme – fitness level 3

	Mon	Tue	Wed	Thur	Fri	Sat	Sun
Week 1		Easy 45 min. ride on flat route	Very hard, hilly 30 min. ride	Easy 45 min. ride on flat route			Easy 60 min. ride on flat route
Week 2		Easy 45 min. ride on flat route	Very hard, hilly 30 min. ride	Easy 45 min. ride on flat route			Easy 60 min. ride on flat route
Week 3		Easy 45 min. ride on flat route	Very hard, hilly 30 min. ride	Easy 45 min. ride on flat route		Very hard, hilly 30 min. ride	Easy 60 min. ride on flat route
Week 4		Easy 45 min. ride on flat route		Easy 45 min. ride on flat route			Easy 45 min. ride on flat route
Week 5		Easy 60 min. ride on flat route	Hilly 45 min. ride	Easy 45 min. ride on flat route			Easy 70 min. ride on flat route
Week 6		Easy 60 min. ride on flat route	Hilly 45 min. ride	Easy 45 min. ride on flat route	Very hard, hilly 30 min. ride		Easy 80 min. ride on flat route
Week 7		Easy 60 min. ride on flat route	Hilly 30 min. ride	Easy 45 min. ride on flat route	Very hard hilly 30 min. ride		Easy 80 min. ride on flat route
Week 8		Easy 45 min. ride on flat route		Easy 45 min. ride on flat route			Easy 45 min. ride on flat route

Sample training programme for fitness level 4

For more experienced cyclists, this plan allows just one day off each week, though Monday is set aside as an easy day. Again, weeks 4 and 8 are set aside for recovery, though they still require at least 150 minutes per week on the bike. As fitness progresses, a rider can still recover from hard training even when required to do sustained endurance rides.

Table 6.5 Sample 8-week programme – fitness level 4

	Mon	Tue	Wed	Thur	Fri	Sat	Sun
Week 1	Easy 30 min. ride on flat route	45 min. hilly	60 min. easy	Very hard 30 min. (or interval training)		45 min. easy	60 min. easy
Week 2	Easy 30 min. ride on flat route	45 min. hilly	60 min. easy	Very hard hilly 30 min. (or interval training		45 min. easy	60 min. easy
Week 3	Easy 30 min. ride on flat route	45 min. hilly	60 min. easy	Very hard hilly 45 min. (or interval training)		45 min. easy	60 min. easy
Week 4	Easy 30 min. ride on flat route	45 min. easy	45 min. hilly	45 min. easy		45 min. easy	45 min. hilly
Week 5	Easy 30 min. ride on flat route	Very hard hilly 45 min.	60 min. easy	Very hard hilly 45 min.		60 min. easy	80 min. easy
Week 6	Easy 30 min. ride on flat route	Very hard hilly 45 min.	80 min. easy	Hard hilly 45 min.		60 min. easy	90 min. easy
Week 7	Easy 30 min. ride on flat route	Very hard hilly 45 minutes	90 min. easy	Hard hilly 45 min.		60 min. easy	100 min. easy
Week 8		45 min. easy		45 minutes easy			60 min. easy

Shift work

Many cyclists are faced with difficulty when trying to fit their training around anti-social and tiring shift patterns in their working lives. The following examples relate to a pattern of 3 days and 3 nights on, and 6 days off. Training during day shifts and days off is deliberately progressive to ensure that recuperation is required while the rider is undertaking night shifts. This means that they do not need to set aside much, if any, training time during this difficult period. The specific details of the easy, medium and hard training sessions would depend on the individual's fitness level.

Table 6.6 Suggested training pattern for shift work

	Mon	Tue	Wed	Thur	Fri	Sat	Sun
Week 1	Night	Night	Night	Off	Off	Off	Off
	Easy	Easy	Easy	Easy	Medium	Hard	Easy
Week 2	Off	Off	Day	Day	Day	Night	Night
	Medium	Hard	Easy	Medium	Hard	Easy	Easy
Week 3	Night	Off	Off	Off	Off	Off	Off
	Easy	Easy	Medium	Hard	Easy	Medium	Hard

Keep a training diary

Try to keep a record of your training – what you have done, as well as what your longer-term intentions are. A daily training log should record anything which is likely to affect your performance – your diet, the quality of the previous night's sleep, the weather conditions, the time of day, your resting and training heart rates, and so on. In this way, exceptional rides (exceptionally bad or good) can be better explained by referring to these various factors in your diary. The example below uses check-boxes to record relevant data quickly and easily, and although it is merely a suggestion, it could be photocopied and used.

Cycling training diary	*Date:*
Resting heart rate (BPM)	
Quality of sleep	
Quality of previous day's diet	
How do I 'feel?' (ranked 1–10)	
Training completed today	
How did I feel during training?	
Was my heart rate responding as I'd expect	
Route details	
Good/bad days training?	
Race notes	

Figure 6.1 Example training diary

Problem-solving

It is more than likely that you will encounter some problems with your training at some point – often through no fault of your own. Perhaps you will find it difficult to fit your exercise in, or difficult to stay motivated. This section will help to identify and address such problems in a positive and practical way.

Time constraints

Fitting your training in around your commitments may be easier if you bear in mind the following advice.

- Communicate your goals to your spouse and discuss how they may affect your relationship and/or family, both positively and adversely.

- Be organised, so that the rest of your life is operating smoothly and all your other responsibilities are being met.

- Try establishing a routine. Many people rise early to train before daily responsibilities begin. The energy gained from regular exercise may compensate for any lost sleep. In fact, exercise might even help you sleep better.

- Try letting something go. Are there low-priority activities you can stop doing to make time for improving your health?

- Pencil in training sessions on your daily calendar. Schedule getting on your bike just as you would any other meeting or obligation.

- Consider lunch-break training. This may help you get the correct amount of training done each week, especially as when you're forced to fit training into an hour and you're not tired from a full working day, you may have the impetus and energy to ride harder. The results should be maximum progress for the time spent. Sandwich short time trials, intervals, sprints and/or climbs between a brief warm-up and cool-down. Of course, to train during lunch you need suitable roads nearby (a park may be available if you work in a city), a facility to shower afterwards, and a safe place to keep your bike. Make up for the missed meal by snacking on wholesome foods, but try to avoid eating within two hours before training (*see* p. 113). You'll probably find you get more work done in the afternoon after an hour of graft in your lunch break.

The 'fitness plateau'

Many riders get to a certain fitness level then fail to see any further improvements. Then it seems that they just can't get faster no matter what they do. The root of the problem is that training, like many things in life, is affected by the 'law of diminishing returns' (*see* fig. 5.1, p. 54). This dictates that initially, upon starting to ride, you will see a slight dip in performance as your body adjusts to regular exercise. Then you will make quite rapid improvements in performance as the training starts to increase your body's efficiency. However, this period of rapid gains can be followed by a period where maximum efforts bring minute improvements or even decreased fitness levels.

The answer is to change – to do things a little differently. The particular thing that you need to change will be specific to you; in other words, individuals suffer this fitness plateau for different reasons. The most likely possibilities are as follows.

- You may not be subjecting your body to sufficient training stress. When you started training, the distances and speeds which you rode each week were probably sufficient to stress your heart, lungs and muscles; therefore, your body adapted to the stress, and your fitness improved. However, if you fail progressively to increase the training load, no adaptation will occur and you will experience no further improvement in your fitness. If you have ridden the same distance at the same speed for the last three months or so you aren't training, just riding your bike. The answer is to step up the overall training volume slightly. Try and do your usual rides in less time. Or take longer rides in the same time period by increasing your training intensity.

- You may be training inconsistently. In other words, perhaps you are training well for a few weeks, having a couple of months off, then training hard again. Just as your body adapts to training, it also adapts to de-training, so that in those couple of months off, you are undoing all your good work. To get consistency into your training, work on a four-week cycle: say, three weeks of consistent rides four times a week, and one week of inconsistent, 'train as you like' rides. That way you will be allowing your body time to recover.

- Another possible cause of fitness stagnation is training too much. Too much can mean too frequently, too fast or too far, or a combination. By training too hard you won't be allowing your body to adapt to the stress of training and to recover sufficiently. If you are constantly tired, irritable, sleeping poorly, and are not seeing an improvement in your fitness, don't train harder – have a rest, then cut down the speed of your rides while maintaining the distances. You should see an improvement in a few weeks. If you are relatively new to cycling, you should also beware of increasing your mileage too quickly. Make sure you have developed a good base fitness, achieved by long slow rides, beforehand (*see* pp. 69–70).

- Next in the list of possible barriers to progress is diet. Training uses energy which must be replaced through diet, and exercise places demands on systems in the body which are regulated by vitamins and minerals. As discussed in Chapter 8, your energy needs will be covered by a balanced diet consisting mainly of carbohydrates such as pasta, rice and potatoes, and vegetables and fruit. Vitamin and mineral needs are a little trickier, since processed food is often lacking these in sufficient quantities. Unless medical reasons dictate otherwise, it is a sensible precaution to use vitamin and mineral supplements. Don't wait until you deplete your energy stores before topping them up; do it on the go, either through solid food or energy drinks (*see* pp. 115–16).

- What is your favourite type of riding: hill climbs, time trials, sprinting? What type of riding do you do most? If the two are the same – which they will be for most of us – then that could be another reason for lack of progress. We tend to concentrate on the things we're good at or like, and avoid the type of training which we aren't so good at. It is just this training that is likely to make us better riders. Try to spend 70% of your training time on the weaker aspects of your riding, and 30% on your strong points. The 30% will maintain your strengths and the 70% will improve your weaknesses. Many riders fall into the trap of undertaking monotonous training sessions because it helped to get them fit in the past. If you have reached your plateau through a steady diet of interval training, then go back to basics with a period of sustained continuous rides – or vice versa. Give your body a shock and force it to adapt to some new stresses.

So far, the problems discussed have involved physical, rather than psychological, barriers to improvement. The latter can, however, be as acute as the former. Perhaps you simply don't think that you will ever get fitter. Prove it then! Give yourself 10 weeks to prove that you'll never get better. Start by getting some measure of your current fitness, say a 10-mile time trial. Then sit down, go through the likely reasons for not having improved in the past, and get down to some serious effort on your bike. (Remember to rest effectively too.) After the 10 weeks, re-run your time trial and marvel at the improvement. In all training it is important to set goals to aim for. Be realistic, and set goals that are attainable, given effort. If your main goal is someway off in the future, set small, short-term goals which, when achieved, will bring the long-term goal closer to hand. Breaking through a plateau can be done by simply taking a fresh approach to your training and adding some new challenges.

Fitness gains without 'training'

It may seem strange that a book on cycling for fitness, written by a cycling coach, could suggest that you can get fit without following a training plan. However, there are many cyclists who are keen on getting fitter through regular riding, but who are not comfortable with going through the process of planning and implementing a specific schedule. This is perhaps understandable, since a written plan may take away some of the pleasure of a lifetime of recreational activity such as cycling. The good news is that you *can* get fitter without training. In reality, this means getting fitter without actually *thinking* that you have been training. You will have been stressing the body and following the principles of training, but in a more relaxed and subtle way than someone who plans things well in advance. While the results will not be optimal, you will still see gains in fitness and as a result you should gain additional pleasure from your cycling, without ever getting too serious.

The following methods of subtle training will help advance your fitness and require only simple adjustments to the cycling which you are already doing.

How can I improve my fitness without a 'training plan'

- *Detour.* If you normally ride over a similar route – and many riders tend to do the same routes regularly – take two detours on each ride. This will add to the duration of the rides, which is one of the components of training overload.

- *Reverse route.* Simply ride your normal routes in reverse. By doing this not only will you get a new perspective on the scenery, but you will probably have a harder ride – increasing the intensity of the ride, another component of training overload.

- *'Out and back'.* Ride away from home for a set time, say 30 minutes, then simply turn around and try and get home in less than 30 minutes. You will be surprised how intense even the most laid-back cyclists become when there is a deadline to beat!

- *Speed burst.* Decide that you will ride much faster than normal until the next red car, next large rock, next farmhouse, next traffic light, and so on – or until you tire; whichever is first. This is an excellent means of adding to the intensity of your rides.

- *The double.* Decide that you are going to ride *twice* as far as your normal route, just to see if you can do it. Don't try to ride very fast, just aim to complete the distance in however long it takes. This is a great way of increasing your total riding duration.

- *Up a gear.* You're riding along in your fourth highest gear. Simply shift on to the next highest, and hold the same pedalling speed for as long as you can. This is another means of increasing the intensity of your rides.

- *Hard hill, easy hill.* On a given day, decide that you will ride hard up all the hills. When it's flat or downhill go extra easily, but when the route points upwards – go for it. The next ride, do the opposite: easy on the hills, and as hard as you can sustain on the flat sections.

- *A hell week.* This is just what it sounds like. For one week, do most of the above. Get yourself well and truly tired and worn out! Then, over the following week, take it easy. Such a hard week will not do any long-term harm, and it comprises a high volume of training stress so that given the easy week which follows, your body will adapt and become stronger and more efficient. Consider it your own little Tour de France! Remember to eat well, drink plenty of fluids and put your feet up when you can.

It is possible to 'trick' your body into getting fitter in a variety of ways. The key to making this method successful is not to do these rides too often, only when you're feeling fresh and with no signs of tiredness. Once a week, and you should see gains.

Motivation

It is sometimes hard to maintain your motivation to train. It can help to make training a habit. Doing things regularly can make difficult tasks easy, but don't become a slave to your schedule. Try the following to keep your training enjoyable.

- *Look at your schedule realistically.* How many days are you willing to commit to an exercise programme? How long per workout? Then write those workout times into your schedule. People often make the mistake of thinking they're going to exercise every day, only to be discouraged and disappointed when they miss a day. More is not necessarily better. The keys to developing a lifetime habit of regular exercise are slow progression, consistency, and regularity. Identify any other obstacles that may prevent you from exercising and find ways in which you might work around them. Try to set aside specific times to ride, and keep these appointments, no matter what. This will give you a sense of responsibility, and give your fitness the priority it deserves.

- *Select an activity that you enjoy,* one that you feel you will want to participate in on a regular basis throughout your life. Forget about logic, and focus on passion. Athletes train day in and day out because they love what they do, not because they have the appropriate gear and enough time or skill. Find something you truly enjoy doing, and there's a greater likelihood you'll stick to it – you've added another dimension than just the exercise.

- *Keep a training diary.* Include activity performed, date, time of day, duration of activity, and how you felt upon completion. This helps to cement your cycling as a habit, rather than a task. If you think of exercise as non-negotiable, like going to work or school, you will just do it, and you're more likely to stay motivated. A lot of people who don't work out on a regular basis have an idea that regular exercisers are always in the mood to work out. This simply isn't true. People who exercise regularly have got into the habit of it, whether they feel tired or not.

- *Top athletes are goal-oriented.* A goal gives you something to work towards, and eventually to reach. Choose something that's both achievable and gives you a sense of triumph in the end. Don't make a 60-mile race your goal if you're just starting to ride. Move too fast, and you're likely to suffer injuries, wear yourself out and lose your motivation. A better approach is to set smaller 'mini-goals' on the road towards your ultimate goal, and give yourself the credit you deserve when you reach them. If you select indoor cycling as your activity and find that you're bored after 10 minutes, start out with 8 minutes per day, three times a week. Gradually add 5 minutes each week.

- *Exercise with a friend.* Friends help to motivate each other and maintain regularity in exercise participation. In order to achieve long-term success, you need to have support. Find a training partner – a friend, a neighbour, an organised group or club – and monitor your progress together. You'll be more likely to stick with your programme if someone is offering encouragement and sharing your pitfalls and triumphs.

- *Reward yourself* after participating in an activity for a certain number of days.

- *Include sufficient rest days in your training.* This will help to avoid injuries and prevent the symptoms of overtraining (for example, illness, tendonitis, severe muscle soreness). Scheduling rest days will not take anything away from your progress. Rather, rest days allow your body to function and make more efficient and rapid progress. You might feel stiff or sore when first starting out, but you should never feel pain. Pain is a signal to the body that something is wrong. If you feel pain or become over-exhausted while training, consult your coach or your physician as appropriate.

- *Finally, don't be afraid to seek advice.* You can never know it all, and the 'expert' whom you approach won't know it all either!

Total body fitness – 'cross training'

Although cycling is a highly effective form of aerobic exercise, bringing a wide range of health and fitness benefits, there are certain aspects of fitness that riding alone cannot fully address. *Flexibility* – or the ability to move joints, and use muscles, through their full range of movement – is one such element and is discussed in relation to 'stretching' in the following chapter.

Another element is *upper body strength*. While mountain biking over extreme terrain will aid its development to a certain degree, the fact is that cycling is primarily a lower-body activity involving mainly the thighs in a rather limited range of movement. For those wishing to gain what could be referred to as 'total body fitness', it is necessary to incorporate other exercise activities (for example, swimming, rowing, running or muscle-conditioning work in the gym) into the weekly cycle training programme. This is sometimes termed 'cross training'.

Some believe that cross training can help achieve a more balanced fitness, which may in itself benefit riding performance. Bearing in mind the principle of *specificity* (*see* p. 59), however, there is strong research to support the fact that at elite level, the athlete seeking optimal cycling performance should focus their efforts on cycle training. However, for the purposes of enhancing all-round, 'health-related' fitness for the novice or relative newcomer, cross training can be both effective and highly enjoyable.

Whatever activities you choose, there are two ways of incorporating them into your overall fitness plan. You can either work out an overall cycle training programme as discussed earlier in this chapter, and replace one or two riding sessions with alternative activities, or you can *add* the extra activities to your programme (in effect training for cycle fitness without compromise but building in extra sessions to enhance your overall fitness). Of course, the second option requires greater commitment in terms of time and effort, and care should be taken not to incur excessive fatigue.

Resistance training programmes

If you prefer to remain a committed cyclist and have no desire to participate in other sports activities, there is one convenient option available to you. A resistance training programme, comprising two or three 20-minute sessions each week, can be highly effective. By keeping the sessions short, there will be minimal impact on your cycle-specific sessions – indeed, they could be scheduled quite feasibly to form part of your pre-ride warm-up or post-ride cool-down. You don't even need access to a gym; many exercises rely on body-weight and the use of everyday objects – such as filled water bottles – to provide resistance. (For ease of reference, these will be called 'weights' in the exercise descriptions below and are shown as dumbells.)

It is not within the scope of this book to discuss in full detail the principles and techniques of resistance training. Any established book on the subject will provide the necessary advice and information. However, the following plan would represent a good base for riders seeking all-round muscular conditioning. Since your normal riding will provide sufficient conditioning of the legs and buttocks, the plan focuses on the upper body – the muscles of the arms, shoulders, chest, and abdomen.

Some upper-body conditioning exercises

The arms – biceps

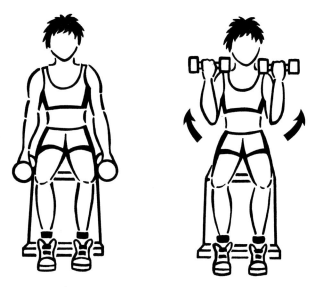

Figure 6.1 Biceps curl

Positioning
Stand, or sit in a sturdy, stable, arm-less chair. With your feet shoulder-width apart, arms fully extended downwards, hold a weight in each hand, palms facing inwards towards your body. *See* fig. 6.1.

The exercise ('biceps curl')
Bending the arm at the elbow, lift the weight almost to the shoulder, slowly and smoothly. While lifting, rotate the palm so that it is facing the shoulder at the top of the movement. Slowly return to your side, and repeat. To save time the exercise can be done lifting both arms at the same time, but remember to maintain the correct technique.

The arms – triceps

Figure 6.2 Triceps kickback

Positioning
Hold a weight in one hand. Bend forwards from the waist until your chest is parallel to the floor, placing your other hand and knee on a bench for stability (*see* fig. 6.2). Your back should be flat and horizontal. Then bend the arm holding the weight 90° at the elbow, and bring it up so that the upper arm is parallel to and close to the side of your body. The weight should be hanging straight down below the elbow.

The exercise ('triceps kickback')
Keeping your elbow still, extend your arm backwards until it is straight and horizontal. Hold for a count of two, then slowly return to the starting position. Repeat. Make sure that you don't swing the weight, and that you keep your upper arm fixed and your lower back flat and still. Use a relatively light weight until you are confident in your technique. Repeat on the other side.

The arms and shoulders – triceps and deltoids

Figure 6.3 Shoulder press

Positioning
Sit on an upright bench, angled at about 90° (or on a suitable chair), so that your lower back is firmly in contact with it. Hold a weight in each hand, hands facing forwards and level with your shoulders. *See* fig. 6.3.

The exercise ('shoulder press')
Press the weights directly upwards over your head. As you straighten your arms, make sure that you don't lock your elbows – they should be 'loosely straight'. Lower the weights slowly back to the starting position and repeat.

The shoulders – deltoids

Figure 6.4 Lateral raise

Positioning
Stand with feet hip-width apart. Hold a weight in each hand. Bend forwards slightly and bring the weights in front of your thighs – the hands should be facing each other. *See* fig. 6.4.

The exercise ('lateral raise')
Raise the weights out to the sides. At the same time, turn your hands so that they face the floor. Raise the weights until your elbows and hands are level with your shoulders. Slowly return to the start position, continuing to resist the weight on the way back down.

The abdominals – rectus abdominis (upper part)

Hands on thighs

Hands across chest

Hands on side of head

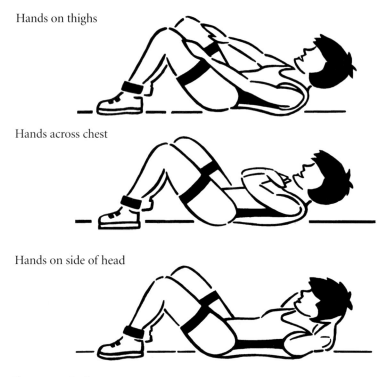

Figure 6.5 *Curl-ups*

Positioning
Lie on the floor, knees bent and feet flat on the floor, hip width apart. Place your hands on your thighs. Make sure your back isn't 'hollow'; there should be a small gap between your lower back and the floor. *See* fig. 6.5.

The exercise ('curl-ups')
Breathe in. Then, as you breathe out, pull your abdomen in and slowly round your spine forwards. Lift your head, shoulders and upper back off the floor. Hold for a count of two, then slowly lower to the ground. Repeat.

As an alternative you may wish to use the other positions shown in fig. 6.5 (hands across chest, or hands on side of head).

The abdominals – obliques (these wrap diagonally around the waist)

Figure 6.6 Lying side-bends

Positioning
Lie on your right side with your knees slightly bent. Place your left arm behind your head. *See* fig. 6.6.

The exercise ('lying side bends')
Raise your head and shoulders slightly off the floor, breathing out as you do so. You should be 'aiming' your ribs at your top hip. Hold this position for a count of two, then breathe in as you return slowly to the starting position. Repeat on your left side.

The back – spinal extensors

Hands on buttocks

Hands on side of head

Figure 6.7 Back extensions

Positioning

Lie face down on the floor, with your hands either on your buttocks, or by the sides of your head, with your elbows out to the sides. *See* fig. 6.7.

The exercise ('back extensions' or 'hyperextension')

Raise your head, shoulders and upper chest slowly from the floor. (Do not raise more than 12 cm from the floor.) Hold for a count of two and then lower gently back. Make sure you keep your legs relaxed on the floor, and only raise as far as is comfortable.

The chest – pectorals

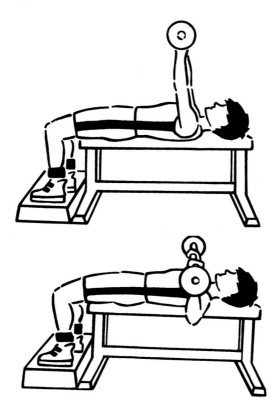

Figure 6.8 Bench press

Positioning
Lie flat on a bench, holding a weight with palms facing forwards and arms fully extended – positioned directly over your chest as shown in fig. 6.8.

The exercise ('bench or chest press')
Slowly lower the weight down to the armpit area. Hold for a moment, then press the weights smoothly back to the starting position.

Planning your session – some useful tips

For the first session, take each exercise in turn and do as many repetitions as you can – always maintaining the correct technique. For example, say you can do 30 shoulder presses. Then work out what 80% of this maximum is: $30 \times 0.8 = 24$ repetitions. Using this figure for each exercise, start your resistance training programme. Try to select a weight or resistance that will allow a maximum of 20–30 repetitions for each exercise. This will ensure that your session will develop strength and muscle tone.

Work through each exercise, doing the correct number of repetitions for your 80% figures. When you have done each of the exercises you have completed a full 'set'. Rest for five minutes then do another set. If you feel comfortable, rest for another five minutes, and do a third. This would complete your session.

Remember to re-test yourself every four weeks or so, and re-calculate your 80% figures again so that you can maintain sufficient training stress on the muscles. Failure to do this will mean that muscle fitness will be maintained at the level you reach in 4–6 weeks after starting, rather than further enhanced as time goes on. Progression can be achieved through a variety of ways:

- a gradual increase in the number of repetitions using the same weight

- the same number of repetitions using a heavier weight

- for maximum training effect, an increase in repetitions using a heavier weight.

Within just a few months, you will notice that your upper body will be much better toned and your muscles should tire much less easily when cycling.

Know your body

One of the keys to successful training is knowing your body – how it reacts to certain types of training or races, its optimal diet, when to train and when to have a break, and so on. Generally speaking, it takes athletes a few years to develop an intimate knowledge of their body. They learn to sense the condition of their muscles, to assess how much sleep they need, to decide whether or not their diet is good enough. You must do the same. Look out for signs of overtraining such as insomnia, loss of appetite, loss of enthusiasm and irritability. Some mornings you will be able to tell if a hard ride is possible just by the feeling in your legs while you are still in bed.

Learning what your body is saying is one thing; doing what it says is another. If you feel lousy, why ride? If you feel great, replace a planned easy ride with a hard interval training session. Don't be a slave to your training plan – learn to be flexible. The progressive cycle of stress, recovery and adaptation is not fixed to any timescale you'll read in this or any other book. It will take time and experience to learn when you have recovered.

Overtraining

The feeling of fatigue that follows a good ride or workout tells you that you are pushing your physical limits, and this is a necessary part of improving personal performance. However, in certain circumstances, fatigue may also be the only warning that you are pushing too hard and need to 'back off' or risk deterioration in performance – or even illness.

There are four levels of fatigue which are experienced by the regular cyclist.

Four levels of fatigue

(1) The fatigue that accompanies energy depletion or dehydration develops 1–2 hours into a strenuous ride, unless you eat regularly on the bike or extend your internal muscle energy stores.

(2) Normal post-exercise fatigue tells you that you are pushing your normal training limits. This will lead to improved performance once you have recovered.

(3) The fatigue that you feel at the end of a particularly hard week of riding (really, a more extreme form of post-exercise fatigue) will – with recovery – also make you faster and stronger. Exercise physiologists refer to this as 'over-reaching'.

(4) Finally, and the one you must try to avoid, the debilitating and long-term fatigue which degrades performance and is the most common symptom of overtraining. It can last weeks or months, and is also commonly accompanied by immune system deterioration and illness.

The challenge for you when building your personal training programme is to find your own limits – in other words, to separate over-reaching and overtraining. Here's how to tell if you may be exercising too much:

- you wake up in the morning and you feel you have not slept enough, even though you may have had seven to eight hours of uninterrupted sleep

- you lose interest in social activities and sex

- you are short-tempered and irritable, get distracted, and lack patience in your day-to-day activities

- you feel like you need coffee or some other stimulant to give you the energy to get through your next workout

- you wonder if it is all worth it to feel this way.

These are all warning signs that your rest to training ratio may be getting out of balance. If you feel that your exercise habits could be out of hand, talk to someone you feel comfortable with, such as your doctor, a family member or friend, a professional counsellor, or someone from your social group. Keep in mind that too much exercise does not necessarily make you look better or get stronger. In some cases it can 'flatten out' your muscles and make you more susceptible to injuries and illness.

Rest and recovery

Most training programmes include at least one (and sometimes two) rest days per week, as well as a day or two of easy spinning. This reflects the practical experience of coaches who have had to deal with the results of pushing too hard for too long. Over-reaching is a normal part of the training cycle, but if your performance is not improving after a few days of recovery, it's time to switch to other aerobic activities which will keep you within your training zone. This will maintain your level of cardiovascular fitness, without the risk of entering the zone of overtraining from which you may take a month or two to recover.

How long do you need to rest? Studies have indicated that recovery from over-reaching (and again, this means keeping your general level of aerobic activity at around 70% max, not complete inactivity) may take up to two weeks with performance improving daily. The implication of this observation is that a one- to two-day taper before a big event may not be enough for you to perform at your personal best. As in all aspects of personal training, there is individual variability; so it is up to you to decide where to draw your own line. But remember that rest is a key part of any training programme and may be the most important choice you'll have to make.

Finally, don't forget to pay particular attention to post-exercise carbohydrate replacement. Part of the fatigue of overtraining may be related to chronically inadequate muscle glycogen stores from poor post-training-ride dietary habits. For more information, *see* Chapter 8 p. 114.

⑦ Stretching and massage

General considerations

Stretching and massage help you adapt to the rigours of cycling. In addition to enabling a faster recovery and lessening the chances of injury, stretching can also help you to produce more power from your muscles. (Unfortunately, one of the problems with hard riding is gradual loss of muscle elasticity and an overall decrease in joint flexibility.) Since stretching improves flexibility and increases range of motion, well-exercised muscles and joints will undergo less severe stress in extreme training conditions. The longer muscles and joints can perform without failure under stress, the longer you can cycle at your optimum speed. The stiffness and tightness frequently felt after a ride can be brought under control, and even eliminated, with proper stretching after a long or intensive training session or race.

The key muscle groups for a cyclist to work on in stretching sessions are those most used. Crucial is the hamstring, or back of the thigh, since any tightness there may transfer tension to the knees or lower back. Then follow the quadriceps (front of the thigh); the inner thigh; the hip flexor; the calves (both gastrocnemeus and soleus), the shoulders; the upper and lower back; the triceps; the pectorals; and the neck. Figure 7.1 illustrates these main muscles or muscle groups, and specific stretches are given on pp. 97–103.

A slow, static stretch that allows the muscle to relax gradually is the safest course of action. Muscles are equipped with a safety mechanism called the *stretch reflex*. If lengthened too quickly or forcefully, they respond with a reflexive contraction which shortens them in a protective reaction. As a result, they are tightened rather than relaxed. To get the most out of your stretch, begin the exercise gently and hold it in place. The essence of stretching is to lengthen the muscle *only* to the point of gentle tension. This is an excellent time to listen to your body; stretching should never cause pain, especially joint pain. If it does, you are stretching too far, and you need to reduce the stretch so that it doesn't hurt (although mild discomfort or a mild pulling sensation is normal).

Warm-up stretches, performed before a training session, should comprise three 'efforts' of 10-second holds per muscle or muscle group. To return muscles to their natural length after your workout, hold the stretch for approximately 20 seconds; do two 'efforts' like this for each muscle or muscle group. This will relax the muscle from the repeated contractions of exercise, thus helping to prevent injury. To actively increase your flexibility, try to follow a pattern of once per day, three days a week, 3 × 20 seconds per muscle or muscle group, with 20-second rests between stretches. Always remember to stretch only to the point of comfortable tension and stop immediately if you feel any pain in joints or muscles.

Superficial muscles

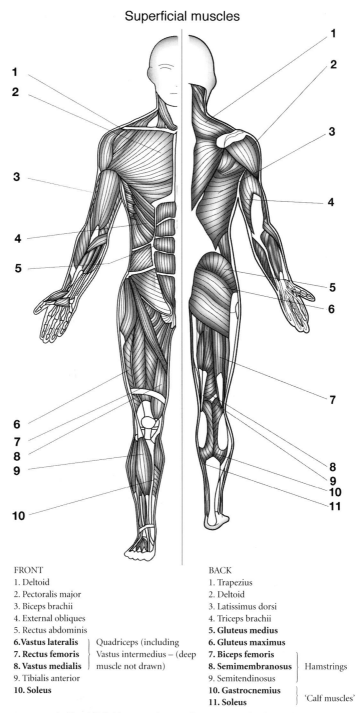

FRONT
1. Deltoid
2. Pectoralis major
3. Biceps brachii
4. External obliques
5. Rectus abdominis
6. Vastus lateralis ⎫ Quadriceps (including
7. Rectus femoris ⎬ Vastus intermedius – (deep
8. Vastus medialis ⎭ muscle not drawn)
9. Tibialis anterior
10. Soleus

BACK
1. Trapezius
2. Deltoid
3. Latissimus dorsi
4. Triceps brachii
5. Gluteus medius
6. Gluteus maximus
7. Biceps femoris ⎫
8. Semimembranosus ⎬ Hamstrings
9. Semitendinosus ⎭
10. Gastrocnemius ⎫ 'Calf muscles'
11. Soleus ⎭

Note: Muscles shown in bold type are those used most extensively when cycling.
Those not in bold are referred to in strength training and stretching exercises in Chapters 6 and 7.

Figure 7.1 Major muscle groups used in cycling

Deep, rhythmic breaths help relax both muscles and minds. When starting a stretch, take a deep breath in and slowly release it as you gradually relax into the stretching position. During the stretch, close your eyes and focus on your breathing. Then, at the point where tension in the muscle begins to release, take another deep breath, filling your lungs and expanding your diaphragm. As you slowly exhale, relax further into the stretch and feel the tension in the muscle melt away.

In addition to stretching during each and every warm-up and cool-down for training purposes, you should include a separate, dedicated stretching session at least once a week. Do a full set of stretches for each part of the body mentioned above. Bear in mind that you need to warm up before these sessions also; a little bit of easy walking or cycling will be sufficient. Never 'bounce' into a stretch; maintain slow, steady movements. Jerking into position can cause muscles to tighten, possibly resulting in injury. Avoid locking your joints into place when you straighten them during stretches – maintain a very slight bend in them.

The stretches

Hamstrings

The muscles in the back of the thigh. These are very important to cycling, since they are active when returning the pedal to the start of the 'power' phase of pedalling.

Positioning

Sit on the floor with your back and shoulders straight. Your right leg should be straight out in front of you, toes pointing up, and your left leg bent out at the side, foot flat on the floor as shown in fig. 7.2. Your hands can be held behind your back to support the spine, or on the outstretched leg as shown.

Figure 7.2 Hamstring stretch

The stretch

• Lean forward from your hips (not your waist) until you feel a stretch in your right leg.

• Keep your back and shoulders straight.

• Hold this position for 15–30 seconds.

• Repeat with the other leg, reversing the position shown in fig. 7.2.

• Repeat the stretch three to five times on each side.

Quadriceps

The muscles in the front of the thigh – the most active muscles used for cycling. They act to straighten a leg bent at the knee, which, for the cyclist, results in the pedals being pushed down powerfully.

Figure 7.3 Front of thigh quadriceps stretch (lying)

Positioning

Lie on your right side, on the floor. Your hips should be aligned so that the left one is directly above the right one. Ensure that your lower back is not hollowed. Rest your head on a pillow or your right hand. Bend your left knee, reach back with your left hand, and hold on to your left heel as shown in fig. 7.3. If you can't reach your heel with your hand, loop a belt over your left foot.

The stretch

- Pull slightly on your foot (with your hand or with the belt) until the front of your right thigh feels stretched.

- Hold this position for 15–30 seconds.

- Reverse your position and repeat with the other leg.

- Repeat the stretch three to five times on each side.

- If the back of your thigh cramps during this exercise, stretch your leg out and try again, more slowly.

Calf muscles – gastrocnemeus

The calf muscles are important for cycling, since they maintain the rigidity of the foot on the pedal, and aid in the final phase of the pedal stroke by pushing the toes downwards.

Positioning

While standing, place your hands on a wall with your arms bent slightly at the elbow. Keeping your right knee slightly bent with the toes of your left foot turned inwards slightly – this places emphasis on the gastrocnemeus muscle. Move your left foot back one or two feet. Your left heel should be flat on the floor – *see* fig. 7.4.

The stretch

- The position itself should initiate a stretch in your left calf muscle. This shouldn't feel uncomfortable.

- If you don't feel a stretch, move your left foot further back until you do.

- Hold this position for 15–30 seconds.

- Repeat with opposite leg, then again, three to five times on each side.

Calf muscles – soleus

Positioning

As for gastrocnemeus, above except keep foot in line – don't turn it inwards. This places more emphasis on the soleus. *See* fig. 7.5.

The stretch

- Keeping your right heel and foot on the floor, bend your right knee slightly.

- Repeat with opposite leg; do the stretch three to five times on each side.

Figure 7.4 Calf stretch – gastrocnemeus

Figure 7.5 Calf stretch – soleus

The shoulders

The muscles found in the shoulders are used to stabilise riding position, and allow control of the bike steering.

Figure 7.6 Shoulder stretch

Positioning

Lie on the floor with a pillow under your head, legs straight. (If your back bothers you, you can place a rolled towel under your knees.) Stretch your arms straight out to the side, on the floor. Your upper arms will remain on the floor throughout this exercise. Bend your arms at the elbow so that your hands are pointing towards the ceiling (*see* fig. 7.6).

The stretch

• Let your arms roll backwards slowly from the elbow. Stop when you feel a stretch or slight discomfort, and stop immediately if you feel a pinching sensation or a sharp pain.

• Slowly raise your arms, still bent at the elbow, to point towards the ceiling again.

• Then let your arms slowly roll forwards, remaining bent at the elbow, to point towards your hips. Again, stop when you feel a stretch or slight discomfort.

• Alternate these movements, beginning and ending with the 'pointing-above-the-head' position.

• Hold each position for 15–30 seconds, keeping your shoulders flat on the floor throughout.

• Repeat three to five times.

Hip flexors

The hip flexors are the primary muscles use in the recovery phase of the pedal stroke, pulling the pedal back to the top position.

Figure 7.7 Hip flexors (half lunge)

Positioning

Begin half kneeling, with your right leg in front, as shown in fig. 7.7. Tighten your abdominal muscles, so that your trunk is stabilised. Alternatively, you can support yourself with one hand on a stool.

The stretch

• Press your right leg forwards, forcing your left hip into extension.

• Repeat on the other side with your left leg in front.

Hip adductors

These muscles are important for positioning the body especially when riding off-road on technical trails. They also stabilise the legs as they travel through the normal pedalling action.

Positioning

Standing sideways on to a waist-high object, place your right foot up on it (*see* fig. 7.8). For stability, you can hold on to something throughout the movement.

The stretch

- Ensure that your toes are pointing forwards.

- Laterally flex your trunk towards the right side (as indicated by arrow).

- Your upper arm must reach towards your foot – not press downwards on the outside of the knee, because this can stress the joint.

Figure 7.8 Hip adductors

Lower back

The lower back muscles are used primarily to stabilise the lower body in the saddle, and they also function as shock absorbers during off-road cycling.

Positioning

As shown in fig. 7.9, lie on the floor with your knees drawn up to your chest.

The stretch

- Grip your knees.

- Pull them into your chest and up towards your shoulders. This should create a 'rocking' movement in the lower spine. To achieve the correct stretch, make sure that you pull the knees to the shoulders and not simply the chest.

Figure 7.9 Lower back

Upper back (rhomboids and thoracic spine)

The upper back muscles aid positioning on the bike which is important for clear vision and bike control.

Positioning

As shown in fig. 7.10, sit on a bench or chair with both arms across your chest. Place your hands on your shoulders.

The stretch

- With both hands firmly on your shoulders, perform a 'flexing' movement to stretch the thoracic spine.

- Be careful not to over-stretch, since this area is often too flexible ('hyper-flexible').

Figure 7.10 Upper back

Triceps

The triceps are responsible for supporting the weight of the upper body on the handlebars, and for pulling on the handlebars when lifting out of the saddle.

Positioning

Stand with your feet hip-width apart, with your left hand over your left shoulder in the centre of your back. Place your right hand at your left elbow, as shown in fig. 7.11.

The stretch

- Use your right hand to ease your left arm further back, using a gentle pressure on the left elbow.

- Repeat on the other side.

- Ensure that you keep your knee joints loosely straight, and don't hollow your lower back. This can be avoided by tucking in your buttocks and tightening the abdominal muscles.

- Stretch only to a point where gentle tension is felt at the back of your upper arm.

Figure 7.11 Triceps

Pectorals

These muscles are used primarily for upper body support. You will use them more when taking part in off-road cycling events.

Positioning

Stand with your feet hip-width apart, arms down by your sides. (You can also perform this stretch seated, with your hands on the floor behind your back.)

The stretch

- Take your hands backwards slowly, keeping your arms loosely straight, until you feel a stretch at the front of your chest.

- You can place your hands on your buttocks, or clasp them together behind your back, depending on comfort.

- To increase the stretch, squeeze your shoulder blades together and lift your chest.

Figure 7.12 Pectorals

Massage

The primary aim of massage is to aid recovery by stimulating blood flow through the muscles. This drains away the toxic by-products of exercise through the lymphatic system, and helps to re-align tangled or knotted muscle fibres. Because the technique is always to rub towards the heart, massage replicates the pumping action of active muscles which 'shunt' blood back to the heart through one-way valves in the veins.

It's worth giving massage a go, even if you're inexperienced. If nothing else, a good rub will help you to relax after a hard ride – as long as you don't dig too deep into sore muscle. If you've always wondered why many cyclists shave their legs, one massage will answer the question. The rubbing goes against the direction of hair growth and is quite painful without smooth legs and some kind of lubrication.

Massage technique

- Start with the front of the thigh, using the thumb and fingers to gently massage each muscle.

- The circulation through the knee can be stimulated using the thumbs in a circular motion, slowly working around the edge of the kneecap. Be careful not to dig too deep into the joint.

- Move on to the shin, stroking the muscles on either side of the shin-bone upwards towards the knee.

- Rubbing hard from side to side across the calf muscles, rather than along the length of them, helps to loosen them prior to stroking actions later in the massage.

- Move on to the back of the thigh, rubbing gently from the knee to the hip.

- Try a 'kneading' action, followed by stroking.

- Move back to the calves again, using the fingers to smooth out the muscle, and running the palm of the hands down the length of the muscles.

- Gentle 'kneading' by the thumb and forefinger on the Achilles tendon increases blood flow through the tendon, which is usually much less than the blood flow through muscle.

- Finish off using flushing strokes along the full length of the legs, back then front.

Some useful massage tips

- Use oil or cream to aid smooth rubbing.

- Rub towards the heart, then glide back to start the next rub.

- Don't massage over injuries, this is for experienced therapists only.

- Stay warm.

- If you're massaging yourself, prop your feet on a chair, and bend your knees so that you can reach the calves and back of the thighs.

8 Fuel for fitness

It may seem that many cyclists – indeed, many sportspeople – have an unusually close relationship with food. Indeed, many a cyclist would proclaim that the best thing about cycling regularly is that it allows them to eat more than they normally could without gaining weight! That aside, if you take the right approach to what and how much you eat, you can see dramatic improvements in both your health and your performance – even without any change in your training habits.

The nutrients that we gain from food perform several functions: energy provision; tissue building and repair; and regulation of the body's functions. For example, carbohydrates give energy, proteins are largely responsible for building and repairing tissue, and fat supports vital organs and acts as an energy reserve. No nutrient acts independently of the others: they must all be present in your body for you to function well. Your diet must be suitably varied to provide all the nutrients you need for normal living and sports training. It isn't enough just to eat a small section of foods which you know are healthy, you need to eat a wide variety of healthy foods. For example, baked potatoes are a good source of energy, but eating nothing but baked potatoes wouldn't provide all of the necessary vitamins, minerals, fats and proteins required for optimal health, let alone for training performance. *Variety* and *balance* are the keys to a healthy diet. The six essential dietary components are *water, protein, carbohydrate, fat, vitamins* and *minerals*.

Water

The condition of the body, its performance, and its ability to resist injury is to a great extent dependent on an adequate fluid intake. Adults differ in the amount of water they carry in the body due to basic body composition. The water 'content' of men ranges from 47% to 65%; that of women, from 43% to 63%*. The reason for the difference is that most men carry more lean muscle mass than most women, and the leaner the body, the more water it carries.

Dehydration occurs when you do not drink enough fluid to replace all that is lost through perspiration, respiration, urination and other body processes. Approximately 3 litres are lost each day under normal conditions, and during prolonged exercise, 1–2 litres of water an hour can be eliminated through sweating. There is no built-in alarm clock within the body that tells you when dehydration is taking place. Thirst is not a sufficient indicator, since you can feel thirsty in a state of adequate hydration, and vice-versa. When you are dehydrated, your blood is more

*R.J. Shephard *et al.* 'Endurance in Sport', in R. Shephard (ed.) *Olympic 'Encyclopaedia of Sports Medicine*, Vol 2, Blackwell Scientific, Boston (2000)

'concentrated', and as such is more susceptible to clotting and less able to deliver oxygen to the brain and muscles. Cooling of the body – effected primarily through sweating – cannot take place without sufficient amounts of water. The digestive system is less efficient and the joints of the body are not properly lubricated. Dehydrate a muscle by only 3%, and you cause about a 10% loss of strength and an 8% loss of contraction speed.

Body fluid can be replaced via any drink including milk, fruit juices and vegetable juices, and through many of the foods we eat. However, plain water is best. Coffee and tea are poor choices because they act as diuretics, stimulating further water loss. Cold water – below 60° – is absorbed faster than room temperature water, leading to faster fuel delivery. It also supplies a reservoir of cold in the stomach that absorbs body heat; this reduces core body temperature and thus aids performance. Later in this chapter the role of fluid intake before, during and after training will be explored. At these times optimal hydration can make the difference between riding for fitness gains and simply riding. As a rule, daily fluid intake (excluding fluids used when riding) should be in the region of 2–3 litres. As a rough guide to ensure optimal hydration levels, 5–6 glasses of water per day should be consumed on top of any other drinks.

Protein

Protein makes up the second largest part of the body, after water. Protein is the major source of building material for internal organs, muscle, blood, skin, hair and nails. Protein is also needed for the formation of hormones, enzymes, and antibodies. Every cell in the body contains some protein.

The body continues to repair itself 24 hours a day. This requires that protein be in the bloodstream at all times for optimum health. A complete protein consists of 22 'building blocks' known as 'amino acids'. Eight of these are considered 'essential amino acids'. If any one of these eight essential amino acids is not in the foods you eat, the body will suffer from a protein deficiency – in effect, it will 'cannibalise' itself by burning protein stored in the muscles to protect the heart, kidneys and other vital organs. Such is its importance in the diet that unlike carbohydrates and fats, you could live on protein alone. You can burn all three for fuel, but only protein can also be used for muscular growth and repair.

Those involved in heavy exercise or hard manual labour need more protein each day than a relatively sedentary person; as a general rule the recommended protein intake for regular exercisers ranges from 1 gram to 1.5 grams per kilogram of body weight. So a 70 kg cyclist should aim to consume 70 to 105 grams of protein daily. As there are 4 calories to 1 gram of protein, this equates to 280–420 calories. As the body can break down fats and carbohydrates faster than protein as a fuel for the body, protein is not normally used as a fuel supply unless insufficient fats and carbohydrates are present in the diet.

Proteins containing all of the eight essential amino acids can be found in both animals and plants. One source is no better than another. Good sources of protein are meat, cheese, milk, fish and eggs. Other important sources are beans, peas and soya beans. Vegetable proteins such as lentils, dried beans, peas, nuts and cereals are considered 'incomplete' proteins because one or more of the essential amino acids is missing; only by combining several of them at the same time will you get a complete protein. Remember that many protein-rich sources are also high in saturated fat (*see* p. 106), so it is advisable to obtain as much of your protein requirement as possible from vegetables, fish and white meat, with lean cuts of red meat and reduced fat dairy produce as second choice.

Carbohydrates

Carbohydrates are the major dietary energy source for most adults, providing fuel for muscle activity and brain function. They yield 4 kilocalories of energy per gram, the same as protein (fat yields 9 kcal/g), and between 40% and 60% of the daily energy 'replacement' calories in a typical 'western' diet. The body will burn protein and fat as energy fuel when necessary, but – due in part to ease of digestion – 'prefers' carbohydrates, especially at the exercise intensities most common to general fitness training.

Carbohydrates can be divided into two types. 'Simple' carbohydrates, such as table, fruit and milk sugars, are very small molecules made up of one or two sugar units. 'Complex' carbohydrates (such as starch) are found in potatoes, brown rice, dried beans, fresh fruits and vegetables, and wholegrain breads and cereals, and are much larger molecules, made up of multiple sugar units joined together. During digestion, all carbohydrates are broken down into single molecule units (mostly glucose, or blood sugar), absorbed, and circulated in the blood to the body cells. Simple carbohydrates are broken down very quickly; complex ones are 'time released', or broken down more slowly so that limited amounts of glucose are in the bloodstream at any one time.

Any excess glucose is stored in the liver and muscles as glycogen (a large molecule, similar to starch and made up of many glucose units joined together) and is available for future energy needs. However, the body can only store a limited amount, around 1600–2000 kcal – enough to last an average person roughly one day if they were to eat nothing.

Research suggests that 60–65% of your total daily calorific intake should come from carbohydrates. Complex carbohydrates should make up the majority of the carbohydrate requirement. As well as providing a good nutritional 'package', these foods also contain dietary fibre, an important element in regulating bowel function.

The amount of carbohydrate that you should eat daily is closely linked to the number of calories you need to take in each day in order to maintain your weight. As a rough guide, active women require between 1600 and 2200 calories daily, whereas active men need between 2800 and 3200 calories a day. It is advisable for women to aim for 6 to 9 servings from the bread group, 3 to 4 servings from the vegetable group, and 2 to 3 servings from the fruit group daily. Active men can eat around 11 servings from the bread group; 5 from the vegetable group, and 4 from the fruit group. Both men and women should have up to 3 daily servings from the milk group – another good source of carbohydrates (*see* fig. 8.1, p. 110, the food pyramid for more details).

During training or competitive events, the body draws heavily from muscle glycogen for its energy supply. As glycogen reserves fall, there is increasing dependence on absorbed glucose circulating in the blood stream. Glycogen depletion can occur in response to repeated near-maximal bursts of effort (interval training) or during sustained endurance exercise. The result can be poor performance levels and fatigue. A common sign of glycogen depletion is difficulty in maintaining normal exercise or performance levels. As mentioned above, for recovery, simple sugars replenish glycogen stores much more quickly than complex carbohydrates.

Fats

Body fat and body composition

The body is made up of two elements: 'lean body tissue', which includes muscle, bone and blood; and 'body fat' (sometimes called adipose tissue). The proportion of the two elements within the body is known as *body composition*.

There are three main types of body fat.

- *Essential fat.* This is vital for survival. It includes the fat surrounding organs such as the heart and kidneys, which insulates and protects them from damage; and the fat which helps to make up cell membranes, the brain and bone marrow.

- *Sex-specific fat.* In women, this is stored mainly in the breasts and around the hips, and ensures normal hormone balance and menstruation. In men it is stored mainly around the waist.

- *Storage fat*, which is an important energy reserve providing 9 kcal/g – over twice as much as both carbohydrate and protein. Of the three fuel sources, fat is the most economical so that during long day tours, ridden at a relatively low intensity, it will be a major energy provider. It is most commonly used as fuel when the intensity is below 50% maximum aerobic capacity.

As well as being an important energy source, the third type of fat is the one which most people worry about. Present in excess, it forms a potentially serious health risk. Research has linked a number of diseases to obesity, including heart disease, diabetes, gall bladder disease, and hypertension (high blood pressure). Excess body fat also tends to adversely affect self-image, and almost always detracts from sports and fitness performance. A healthy body fat percentage is around 13–18% for men and 18–25% for women. There are several different ways in which body fat can be measured; the most simple is by skinfold measurement using calipers. Most health clubs and sports centres use this method.

It is important to remember that very low body fat levels can be harmful too, increasing the risk of respiratory disease, and certain cancers and metabolic disorders. A minimum body fat percentage of 5% for men and 10% for women is generally considered necessary for basic body function.

Dietary fat

Any excess calories taken into the body are converted into fat. Therefore, it is a general truth that the percentage of fat present in an individual's body is linked directly to their diet.

It is recommended by most government health agencies that fat comprise no more than 30% of one's daily calorie intake. One of the biggest problems in the western diet is that on average, the adult population eats between three and five times the amount of fat needed to keep the body functioning efficiently.

Dietary fats and oils consist mainly of triglycerides, composed of a unit of glycerol and three fatty acids. These fatty acids are classified into two main types, according to their chemical structure: 'saturated' and 'unsaturated'. Of these, it is saturated fatty acids that are most detrimental to health, since they can increase harmful blood cholesterol levels and thus increase the risk of heart disease. They are found mainly in animal products such as butter, cheese and meat fat. Unsaturated fats found mainly in plants and fish, should therefore make up the majority of your fat intake.

In terms of your fat intake, for the purposes of cycling for fitness the important thing to focus on is a balanced and varied diet. If the main aim of your fitness programme is to reduce body fat, a programme of regular aerobic exercise combined with good nutrition should be sufficient for you to see significant progress in a relatively short time (*see also* pp. 110–11 'the food pyramid', and p. 113 for a Sample Daily Diet). At elite levels it becomes necessary to follow a stricter regime; this is covered in more detail in Chapter 9.

Vitamins and minerals

Vitamins

Vitamins act as catalysts for the metabolic processes that convert fats, carbohydrates and proteins into calories – or energy. As such, they facilitate the reaction, but are not 'used up' or consumed by it. Many of the processes which take place in the body during and after exercise are facilitated by vitamins: for example, vitamin E is a powerful anti-oxidant, enhancing recovery after hard exercise and literally preventing disease by protecting cells from free radical 'attack' (*see* p. 111).

If you are concerned about your diet being unbalanced, there is no harm in using a simple, over-the-counter multi-vitamin once a day. However, vitamins are not the easy answer to increased health and fitness.

Minerals

Minerals are chemical elements found in the body either in their elemental form or combined with organic compounds. Like vitamins, they are essential for normal cell functioning. The two most prevalent minerals, calcium and phosphorus, are major components of bone; while sodium and potassium are found in all tissue fluids, both within and around cells.

Magnesium, chloride, sulphur and zinc are other minerals that play a key role in cell function. The trace elements iron, manganese, copper and iodine are found in much smaller quantities, but play essential roles in facilitating basic cellular chemical processes. For example, iron plays a crucial role in the manufacture of red blood cells, which transport oxygen – vital for the proper functioning of active muscle.

In terms of supplementing, the same applies as for vitamins above. Given the fact that modern production methods may adversely affect the content and quality of nutrients present in food, it may well be wise to take a quality supplement as a 'safety net' – unless, of course, you have any medical condition that dictates against it.

Eating to maximise health

Eating more healthily doesn't need to be difficult. A useful means of establishing your daily dietary needs is by using the food pyramid shown in fig. 8.1. This provides a graphic guide for making healthy food choices. The pyramid calls for eating a variety of foods to get the nutrients you need, while eating the right amount of calories to maintain a healthy body weight. Each of the pyramid food groups provides some, but not all, of the nutrients you need. Foods in one group cannot replace those from another. No one food group is more important than any other, but for a balanced diet, those foods at the top should be consumed more sparingly than those at the base (*see* below).

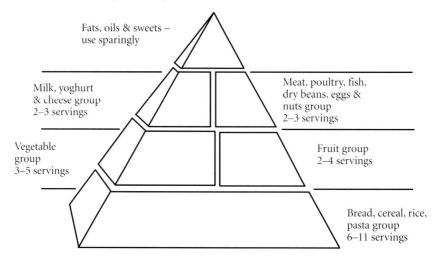

Figure 8.1 The food pyramid

The top of the pyramid

Fats, oils and sugar should be used sparingly in the diet and therefore are represented as the small tip of the pyramid. They are present in salad dressings, oils, cream, butter, margarine, soft drinks, candies and sweet desserts; they provide calories but few or no vitamins and minerals.

The middle of the pyramid

Protein is needed in moderate amounts in the diet and therefore represents the upper middle of the pyramid. Milk, yoghurt, cheese, meat, poultry, fish, dry beans, eggs and nuts are important sources of protein as well as good sources of calcium, iron and zinc. Choose lean meats, skinless poultry, fish and low-fat dairy products to control fat and cholesterol intake. Also, limit breaded or fried foods for the same reason.

Fruit and vegetables can be regarded as helping to form the 'foundation' of the pyramid. Besides being an excellent source of vitamins, minerals and fibre, these plant foods are low in fat and sodium and are free of cholesterol. Eating a variety of vegetables and fruits will help ensure that you meet your daily need for vitamin C – 40 mg per day for both men and women – and other nutrients. You should aim to eat five or more servings of fruits and vegetables every day. To encourage this, make them more visible at home and at work, by keeping a fruit bowl on the kitchen counter or at the office. The following all equate to one serving (the 'cup' measurement is used for simplicity – there is no need to get out the kitchen scales to eat healthily, simply scoop or pour out a cupful as a guide).

- 1 medium fruit or ½ cup of small or cut-up fruit

- ¾ cup of 100% fruit juice

- ¼ cup dried fruit

- ½ cup raw or cooked vegetables

- 1 cup raw leafy vegetables (such as lettuce, spinach)

- ½ cup cooked beans or peas (such as lentils, pinto beans, kidney beans)

Research indicates that people who eat lots of fruit and vegetables may be less at risk from cancer than those who don't. This may be due to their relatively high content of 'antioxidants'. These help the body to deal with, and prevent the excessive formation of, *free radicals* in our system. Free radicals can be described as molecules that have gone 'awry' as a result of oxidised or 'bad' oxygen. They are reactive chemicals capable of randomly damaging DNA and proteins. Exercise that is sufficiently hard to elicit a training response will result in some degree of free radical formation. Vitamins A, C and E form a powerful antioxidant group, and the trace minerals selenium and zinc also play a key antioxidant role.

The base of the pyramid
Bread, cereals, rice and pasta – all foods from grains – are found at the base of the pyramid because they are the foundation upon which the rest of the diet is planned. Try to choose 6–11 servings daily (*see* below). Grains supply fibre, carbohydrates, vitamins and minerals. They are usually low in fat, and are the preferred fuel for our brain, nervous system and muscles. To keep these foods low in fat and calories, e.g. limit the use of spreads on bread.

The cyclist who is training regularly will obviously need to be taking in more calories than a relatively sedentary person, but also needs to increase the consumption of essential endurance-related nutrients such as complex carbohydrates, as well as iron and essential fats. The best of the complex carbohydrates – those which are of greatest benefit – are found in pasta, rice, bread and grains, as well as potatoes from the middle of the pyramid. Try always to go for the wholegrain varieties where possible, since these are an important aid to digestion.

What counts as one serving?

Here are some examples of serving size for each food group. If you eat a larger portion, count it as more than one serving. Try to eat at least the lowest number of servings from the five food groups each day (again, the cup is used as the simplest means of measurement).

Bread, cereal, rice and pasta group (6–11 servings)

- 1 slice of bread
- 1 ounce of ready-to-eat cereal (check labels: 1 ounce = ¼ cup to 2 cups depending on cereal)
- ½ cup of cooked cereal, rice or pasta
- ½ hamburger roll, bagel, wholemeal scone
- 3 or 4 plain crackers (small)

Vegetable group (3–5 servings)

- 1 cup of raw leafy vegetables
- ½ cup of other vegetables, cooked or chopped raw
- ¾ cup of vegetable juice

Fruit group (2–4 servings)

- 1 medium apple, banana, orange, nectarine or peach
- ½ cup of chopped, cooked or canned fruit
- ¾ cup of fruit juice

Milk, yoghurt and cheese group (2–3 servings)

- 1 cup of milk or yoghurt
- 1½ ounces of natural cheese
- 2 ounces of processed cheese

Meat, poultry, fish, dry beans, eggs, and nuts group (2–3 servings)

- 2–3 ounces of cooked, lean meat, poultry, or fish (1 ounce of meat is equivalent to ½ cup of cooked dry beans, one egg or two tablespoons of peanut butter).

Sample daily diet for a cyclist in training

The following sample meals are intended to give you an idea of the correct variety and quantity of food required by a cyclist undertaking regular training. They are not intended to be followed strictly, and may not give you the total calorie intake that you need.

Breakfast
1 cup bran cereal
1 banana
1 tsp margarine
500 ml low-fat milk
1 slice wholemeal bread
250 ml fruit juice

Lunch
150 grams lean meat
2 tsp mayonnaise or mustard
½ cup coleslaw
Lettuce and tomato
1 bread roll
2 oatmeal cookies
1 fresh peach
500 ml water

Dinner
Chicken stir-fry:
    1 cup diced vegetables
    2 cups rice
    1 cup yoghurt
    3 ounces chicken
    2 tsp oil
1 cup orange and grapefruit sections
500 ml fruit juice

Snack
3 cups popcorn
500 ml fruit juice

The vegetarian cyclist

The recommendation of a diet rich in carbohydrate may lead many riders to what is essentially a form of vegetarian diet. A strict vegetarian, known as a *vegan*, eats no animal products at all. Lacto-vegetarians add milk, and other dairy products such as cheese, to their diet. Ovolacto-vegetarians eat both eggs and milk products. Yet another group, which would be called 'semi-vegetarians', avoid red meat such as beef and pork, but eat fish and poultry in addition to their ovolacto-vegetarian diet. Additional emphasis is placed on foods that are 'organic' and unprocessed or unrefined – although of course, this preference is not confined to vegetarianism.

A major concern about vegetarian diets has always been the question of how a balanced intake of nutrients may be ensured. While a lacto-vegetarian or ovolacto-vegetarian diet may meet all nutritional needs, there may be a shortage of iron, calcium, iodine, selenium, zinc, riboflavin, vitamin D and vitamin B_{12} in a strictly vegetarian diet. Iron intake may also be low in a lacto-vegetarian diet, because of the lack of *haeme-iron* from meat sources. This is more easily absorbed than iron from vegetable sources; and in fact aids the absorption of iron from vegetable sources.

To receive a balanced distribution of essential amino acids, the vegetarian must eat foods that possess mutual supplementation of dietary protein. This is a nutritional strategy in which vegetable foods with low contents of amino acids (cereals, for example) are eaten together with a food that is high in that same amino acid (for example, milk or beans). In order to obtain an intake of good quality proteins in the diet, the following food combinations are recommended:

- pasta with cheese;
- rice and milk pudding;
- cereals with milk or egg;
- potatoes with egg or cheese;
- rice and beans;
- lentils and bread.

If care is taken to include a wide variety of foods, and to combine them in an appropriate way, vegetarian diets can be nutritionally adequate and will not impair one's training.

Nutrition for cycle training

Prior to a training session, there are three important questions that the cyclist must consider.

- Am I adequately hydrated?
- Have I enough energy available for the session?
- Has my last meal had time to leave the stomach?

For short (i.e. less than one hour), moderate intensity rides, taking in water will be more than adequate. But if you train hard and often, water won't be enough; you will need to take in additional carbohydrates for 'fuel'. Failure to do so may result in your training at less than optimal intensity, and thus a less effective use of your precious training time.

Snacking of some sort, on solid or liquid food, while on the bike is important. However, as intensity increases above 60%, it becomes more important to avoid eating within two hours of the training session to avoid stomach discomfort. If you're going to be doing intervals it is vital to have your stomach empty or you risk stomach distress. You will also sweat more so that fluid replacement needs to be carried out with special care. Even though you may be spending less time training when doing intervals, a hard interval session of 30 minutes can leave your glycogen stores depleted – so maintain normal energy drink intake and post-training loading (*see* below).

After training comes what is known as the 'glycogen window'. This basically means that post-exercise, your body is much more efficient at replacing the carbohydrate stores which may have been depleted by the training session. Therefore, it is wise to have a carbohydrate snack available immediately after your ride finishes. Eat at least 50 grams of carbohydrate just after exercise, and consume a total of at least 100 grams of carbohydrate in the subsequent 4-hour period. Further carbohydrate intake may be advisable for the next 18 to 20 hours; aim to consume at least 600 grams of carbohydrate during the 24 hours after an intense workout or competition.

A high-carbohydrate diet increases stores of glycogen – the energy for muscles – and improves overall performance. If you exercise for longer than an hour, you can begin to deplete your muscle glycogen stores. By consuming 30 to 75 grams per hour of carbohydrate in liquid or solid form when you exercise, you can minimise this effect. After a long (90 minutes or more) workout or competition, your depleted muscle glycogen stores must be fully replenished, especially if you will be exercising again within the next 12–24 hours.

Hydration for cycle training

You must ensure that you are fully hydrated. Because carbohydrate is stored along with water in the muscle, a high carbohydrate intake with low fluid intake can lead to water being drawn from other tissues, leaving you close to dehydration before the session even starts. Proper fluid replacement before, during, and after training positively influences performance. Maintaining body fluid levels during training becomes especially important when the loss from the skin and expired air exceeds 2 litres per hour, as it often does in hot weather.

Thirst is an unreliable indicator of fluid needs, partly because the intake of water quickly dulls the thirst sensation. Further, hydration with plain water dilutes the blood rapidly and stimulates an increase in urine production – this in turn leads to greater dehydration. Re-hydration will occur more rapidly when drinks containing *sodium* (salt) – the major electrolyte lost in sweat – are consumed. Ingesting a drink containing sodium helps to maintain thirst while delaying the stimulation of urine production. The drink should also ideally contain glucose or sucrose, because these carbohydrates provide a source of energy for working muscles, stimulate fluid absorption in the gut, and improve the taste. The following guidelines will help you maintain proper hydration during training and competition.

Energy drinks

An 'energy drink' is a drink especially formulated for the rapid replacement of carbohydrates and electrolytes – the mineral salts dissolved in the body's fluid – which are lost or used up as a result of intensive exercise. Being mostly water, energy drinks are also useful because they rehydrate the body at the same time. In theory, energy drinks are not needed by cyclists riding at a moderate intensity, and for less than 90 to 120 minutes. Your body has adequate energy stores for that amount of time. However, you'll recover your energy more quickly at the end of the ride if you

Maintaining hydration during training and competition

- Weigh yourself without clothes before and after training and racing, especially during hot weather. For each pound of body weight lost, drink two cups of fluid.

- Use a drink containing sodium to quickly replenish lost body fluids. This drink should also contain 6–8% glucose or sucrose (*see* above).

- Drink 2.5 cups of fluid two hours before training or competition.

- Drink 1.5 cups of fluid 15 minutes before a session or event.

- Drink at least 1 cup (roughly 2 mouthfuls) of fluid every 15–20 minutes during training and competition.

- Do not restrict your normal fluid intake before or during an event.

- Avoid drinks containing caffeine and alcohol, because they increase urine production and lead to further dehydration.

have at least partially replenished those stores en route. Since they are in liquid form, the nutrients in energy drinks begin to enter the bloodstream in as little as 10 to 15 minutes.

Energy drinks help to maintain energy and strength, but many of them also have a diuretic effect which can be a nuisance when riding. They also cause some riders to feel nauseous. It is important to use a drink that you actually think tastes nice, or you won't drink enough and may get dehydrated. The energy drinks that work best have a concentration of 5–8% sugar for optimal absorption. Too much sugar concentration slows down the process, and can cause an energy peak followed by a depression. Fructose can cause stomach upsets and is in any case absorbed slowly. Dextrose and sucrose metabolise more slowly than glucose, but are still relatively quick compared with fructose. Amino acids speed absorption. Sodium and potassium increase water absorption and make the drinks taste better.

Solid food works just as well to keep up energy levels, but the nutrients can take 30 minutes to reach the bloodstream, so one must plan ahead. Plain water – even with a pinch of salt – works just as well to keep the body hydrated. A litre of sports drink costs three times more than a banana, yet delivers approximately the same number of calories from carbohydrate.

Today's energy drink market offers a wide choice of flavours from plain to tropical fruits, and a wide range of ingredients. For the majority of riders, a basic glucose-polymer based drink (a drink which contains lots of simple glucose molecules which can be absorbed into the blood quickly) is more than adequate and provides a cost-effective means of fuelling training rides. The following are fine (prices at time of writing): Maxim (£11.95 per 2000 grams); High5 (£12.99 per 1400 grams).

Cycling and weight loss

If you want to lose weight and keep it off, then it's time for a little 'food focus'. Eating is a big part of our lives, so taking charge of your food choices is crucial for successful weight loss. Some people search for a quick way to lose weight, and fad diets are popular because they promote rapid, temporary weight loss. However, fad diets and crash dieting actually result in loss of lean muscle mass, water and stored energy, not loss of excess body fat. As a result, most people on such diets become fatigued early in the day or, if participating in sport – early in the game and have a hard time finding the energy to play at their full potential.

Calorific requirements differ for everyone and are determined by age, sex, weight and level of activity. Simply put, weight is a matter of balance between calorific intake (in) and expenditure (out). Body weight will change when there is an imbalance between calories in and calories out. To lose weight, intake must be less than expenditure. In short, to lose weight you must eat less or exercise more, or do a combination of both.

To put weight loss in perspective, use the formula below:

3500 calories ÷ 7 days per week = 500 calories per day

Weight loss is most successful when diet and exercise are combined together. Eating 500 calories fewer per day will result in a weight loss of one pound per week. Eating 250 calories less per day combined with a 250-calorie deficit from exercise or training will also result in the same weight loss of one pound per week, however, it will be a healthier, more balanced way of losing weight.

Cycling can be the ideal way to aid your weight loss. When you are doing an activity that you enjoy and can easily incorporate into your life, you'll stay motivated longer. Increasing the intensity of your workouts as you become fitter can only help more. The following are some useful, additional tips.

Additional tips

- Don't restrict your diet too much, or you'll end up feeling deprived. Then you'll be more likely to 'binge' eat, or quit your diet altogether. Plus, if you limit your calorie intake too much, your metabolism will slow down to a crawl and your body will gain weight instead of maintaining it.

- Try to monitor yourself and your habits. For instance, keep a journal of what you eat, where you eat, when you eat, and how you feel when eating. Then you can track the patterns. Recognising your eating habits is the first step towards changing them into new, improved ones.

- Be realistic about your weight-loss goal and the dieting process as a whole. Losing weight takes time.

- Be prepared for the low points by accepting that they will happen. When you feel like you've 'slipped' from your diet, don't immediately conclude that you've failed! Instead, use your energy to get back on track, rather than punishing yourself. By choosing to pursue a healthier weight, you've made a long-term commitment to your health, and your actions over a few days won't change that!

- To lose weight safely and effectively, it is important to eat a wide variety of foods from the Food Pyramid (*see* pp. 110–11), consuming enough high-carbohydrate foods to fuel exercise and lowering fat consumption for calorie restriction, rather than following a very low-calorie-diet.

- Only weigh yourself every two weeks, at the same time of the same day. Weight fluctuates quite a bit. If you weigh yourself every day you may get disheartened.

- Remember, though, that weight isn't an issue. What matters is the amount of fat that you're carrying. Check this by pinching your skin and fat, make mental notes of the size of pinch you can get, and check every couple of weeks. You could actually lose fat but increase weight as you build muscle. So don't be a slave to the bathroom scales.

Part IV

Beyond fitness – training for competition

9 Cycle sport training

Cycle sport in its many forms demands a high degree of efficiency in the various components of fitness discussed throughout this book. If you have developed good endurance, this will enable you successfully to complete almost any form of cycle sport. However, at elite athlete level you will need to move beyond the ability simply to finish an event; you must develop the specific elements of fitness that will allow you to 'compete' within a discipline – rather than just participate.

These fitness elements do not exist in isolation, but rather overlap and interrelate according to the demands of your chosen event. For example, you will need explosive power when attacking; a developed intensity threshold when riding hard in a break; and the ability to maintain speed – requiring a high level of endurance and pain tolerance – as the finish line approaches and your competitors are almost upon you.

Although these terms have been discussed in earlier chapters, it may be helpful to redefine them briefly here in relation to given cycle sport disciplines – see the shaded box below. (Sample training sessions aimed at developing each specific fitness element are given in Tables 9.4–9.10 on pp. 128–30.)

Cycle sport training – the requisite fitness element

- *Aerobic conditioning* (*see also* Table 9.4, p. 128). This is the ability to ride for extended periods at sub-maximal levels; such as during a relatively inactive day spent in the main peloton within a multi-day road stage race, or a 200 km randonnee.

- *Aerobic power*, or VO_2max (*see also* Table 9.5, p. 128). This is the maximum amount of oxygen you can extract from the air and use in the working muscles for the aerobic production of energy. It is particularly relevant to 'high power' endurance work of 3–8 minutes' duration, such as that done by a track rider over a 4000 m pursuit.

- *Intensity threshold* (*see also* Table 9.6, p. 129). The ability to ride at a high percentage of your maximum for sustained periods (more than 20 minutes) without suffering rapid fatigue; for example, during a 40 km time trial.

- *Muscular endurance* (*see also* Table 9.7, p. 129). The ability to sustain repeated muscle contractions at a higher force than is normally required; for example, powering over a short climb in a higher gear than would normally be used.

- *Explosive power* (*see also* Table 9.8, p. 130). The ability to develop near maximal force in a very short time; such as sprinting hard to establish a gap between you and other riders when trying to break away from a group.

- *Pain tolerance* (*see also* Table 9.9, p. 130). The ability to continue a high work rate while suffering pain and discomfort in the propulsive muscles; for example, a track rider sustaining high power for 90 seconds, trying to bridge a 60 m gap in a points race.

This chapter will look at each type of cycle sport in turn, together with the fitness demands that are specific to that sport. It will then explore the ways in which the requisite fitness elements can be trained – both individually and in combination – to form an effective training plan.

Cycle sports – the various disciplines

Road racing

Road racing, mass-start events on roads or paved tracks, encompasses events ranging from 50-minute town centre criteriums (usually a course of one mile or less) to one-day classics over 280 km, and ultimately to the three-week-long 4,500 km Tour de France. Within a given race, the power outputs required can vary greatly. For example, one race might demand 3 hours at 200 watts, repeated 3–4 minute efforts of 500 watts, and a maximal sprint of 1500 watts. In fitness terms, this makes road racing, and the training associated with it, extremely demanding.

Figure 9.1 Road racing

Regular success in road racing will only come to the rider who has developed sufficient specialist fitness to deal with the many variables which the event can throw at them. To a high degree of aerobic fitness – both conditioning and power – should be added: explosive power; muscular endurance; the ability to tolerate pain in the muscles; the ability to burn fat as fuel and conserve carbohydrate stores, thus enabling a rapid recovery; the ability to make, or respond to, repeated attacks; and the ability to ride at 'threshold' (above which level the rider would suffer premature fatigue, *see also* p. 121).

The highly tactical aspect of road racing means that the event is taxing psychologically as well as physically. Typically the heart rate can range from lows of 130 to highs in the 180s. Such variations can be even more extreme during a stage race. In multi-day events consisting of road races, time trials (*see* below) and possibly criteriums as well, a rider can spend time at well below 100 beats per minute while in the centre of a large peloton on 'rest' days, then at near maximal levels during attacks and counter-attacks.

Generally, the longer the road race, the greater the demands in terms of aerobic conditioning and power, with the shorter events such as criteriums demanding greater explosive power and pain tolerance. However, there is no escaping the fact that the successful road racer must possess high levels of each element of fitness: base endurance; aerobic power for more intense, sustained efforts such as short climbs; intensity threshold for time trial stages and lone attacks; explosive power for effective springs and attacks; and pain tolerance for occasional forays over the intensity threshold. Muscular endurance needs to be developed to aid riding in strong winds and on gradual, short climbs when high speeds must be maintained.

Time trials

Time trials require riders to raise their intensity quickly to the 'threshold' level, then attempt to maintain this intensity for the duration of the event. Depending on the length of the event, they may need to work on some specific fitness areas such as pain tolerance or a high aerobic conditioning for 100 mile–24 hour tests.

The time trial rider quickly brings the heart rate up to their threshold level, and maintains this level with occasional deviations caused by inclines and descents. Whilst riding at threshold, cyclists are balancing the production of lactic acid (a by-product of high intensity exercise, relying on carbohydrate metabolism, *see also* pp. 107–8) with its removal from the muscle. If the power output is suddenly increased, they will be unable to remove lactic acid effectively from the muscle and fatigue will set in. They will then be forced to reduce their effort to restore the balance. Effective training will increase the power that can be produced before lactic acid begins to accumulate in the muscle – having made the energy pathways more efficient, increased the blood supply to the muscle (hence aiding removal), and improving the ability of the blood to 'buffer' the effects of high acidity in the muscle.

Attributes such as explosive power and pain tolerance are less essential for the time triallist, who essentially brings his power output up to his threshold, and seeks to maintain it for the duration of the event. The threshold will vary depending on the length of the test, with sustainable heart rates varying by up to 15 beats for 10-mile compared with 5-mile events.

Mountain bike racing

Mountain bike racing has two main branches – cross-country and downhill. The latter involves high speed descents over steep and technical trails, and is largely a power and strength sport – although there is an endurance element. However, downhill racing does require a great deal of skill; more perhaps than any other branch of cycle sport.

Cross-country racing involves sustained, high intensity riding on rough off-road tracks of between 10 and 40 miles. Although it appears to be an extremely arduous sport, it is in fact one of the easiest and most accessible for the novice. It is open to beginners, with special categories for novices; such rides are carried out over the same terrain as for elite riders, but will be much shorter. Bike-handling skills are important, although you can always get off and push if necessary! There is usually a far less intimidating atmosphere at cross-country than at other events and races, and there are rarely any mountains in sight – even city wasteground and urban parkland have been used for international elite races.

Figure 9.2 Mountain bike racing

Track racing

The one factor which separates track from other disciplines is the need to develop a high *cadence* or pedalling speed. This is facilitated by changes in the nervous system's electrical 'drive' to muscles, and can only be trained by many hours of high-cadence riding. A cyclist who spends a lot of time racing on the track at high speed will often find that when they turn to other disciplines such as road racing, they lack higher-end power and strength. This is due to the 'strength-endurance continuum', which in effect means that developing high levels of endurance prevents the development of high levels of strength. Relatively light pedal resistance but high pedalling speed trains more endurance-oriented muscle, leading to a decline in the efficiency of strength-oriented muscle.

Figure 9.3 Track racing

Planning a race training programme

Planning a race training programme involves the same principles that were examined in Chapter 6. The difference is that *specificity* in training becomes rather more important for the competitive cyclist. In addition, training must be planned to ensure that you are free from fatigue on the day of the event. The four main steps in planning a race programme are set out below.

Identify the demands of your chosen event

Take your chosen event and consider the following questions.

- How long does the event last?

- Is the intensity consistent or variable?

- If variable, what is the lowest intensity you will be faced with?

- What is the highest intensity you will be faced with?

- How rapid are the changes in intensity?

- What are all the possible scenarios influencing the result? For example, wind direction and strength could be crucial in a road race; technical (bike control) ability could come to the fore when racing off-road in wet weather; or being drawn against an overly aggressive rider may affect tactics in a track sprint.

Identify your weaknesses and strengths

When do you lose out to other riders in competition? When do you struggle? What types of courses do you dislike? List everything that you feel prevents you from winning.

Then, using a scale of 1 to 10 (1 = very poor, 10 = excellent), subjectively evaluate yourself in respect of the six aspects of cycle fitness given below. It's even worth getting some input from other riders – maybe you're not as great a sprinter as you think! The main thing is to be honest. Generally, if you enjoy something you will be good at it; so if you hate climbing, it's likely that you could make some improvements in that area.

Table 9.1 Identify your weaknesses and strengths (i)

Component	Importance for chosen event (1–10)	Personal ranking (1–10)
Aerobic conditioning		
Explosive power		
Muscle power		
Intensity threshold		
Aerobic power		
Pain tolerance		

Now write down the competitive fitness components where you feel that you are weak (a score of less than 4), and then all those which you feel are your strengths (a score of 8 or more).

Table 9.2 Identify your weaknesses and strengths (ii)

Component	Bad at (less than 4)	Good at (8 or more)
Aerobic conditioning		
Explosive power		
Muscle power		
Intensity threshold		
Aerobic power		
Pain tolerance		

Identify your training opportunities

Next, you must consider how much time you have to train each week. Be honest, and don't forget to include the time that it takes to get ready for a ride, to warm up and cool down, and to change and shower afterwards.

Table 9.3 Identify your training opportunities

	Mon	Tues	Wed	Thurs	Fri	Sat	Sun
Time (mins)							

Plan your programme

Now that you've worked out when you'll train, and what aspects of fitness you wish to improve, you can start to put it into the larger perspective of races or major rides. To improve fitness and speed you need to stress the body, allow time for it to adapt to the stress, then stress it again. A potential problem with the need for training overload is the mere fact that the human body is so able to adapt to the stresses imposed upon it during training. For elite cyclists, this can mean increasing training stress levels to such a height that the body's power of recovery simply can't 'keep up'. Training must therefore be redesigned to target weak points, and to focus on one physiological system or structure while another is recovering. For example, when tired from a high-intensity interval training session, a low-intensity continuous ride can often be scheduled the next day without adversely affecting recovery.

Ideally, you want to race after a period of adaption, since the body's various systems will be recovered and at optimal capacity – energy levels will be high, muscle structures will be repaired and everything will be ready for action. Work your body hard during periods when there are few important races, and ease off to allow adaption in the lead-up to races. If you have races marked up it's easier, starting a build-up and recovery phase weeks before the race. You can also do this before big day trips and tours. Too many riders train hard right up to a race, do badly, get fed up, stay off the bike for a few days, then get back on and feel 110%. They had their recovery phase after the race, rather than before.

In general, spend 20% of your time working on your strengths and 50% of your time on weaknesses (with 30% on everything else). This should result in improvements in all aspects of your riding, but will specifically aim towards eliminating weaknesses.

Some sample training sessions

The following sample training sessions are intended as a guide to improving the fitness elements that are specific to your chosen cycle sport discipline (*see also* pp. 122–25). They can be used to help build on your strengths, and to eliminate weaknesses. In conjunction with the general advice given above, on planning a race training programme, such sessions will help to provide a solid base for competition.

Table 9.4 Sample sessions to train aerobic conditioning

Components of session	Aerobic conditioning		Comments
	Sample 1	Sample 2	
Intensity	65% max. heart rate range	75% max. heart rate range	For this – your main endurance session – you should aim to balance the intensity to enable you to complete the ride. Try not to start off too hard – as a rough guide, the first third should feel comfortable, the middle third 'uncomfortable', and the final third hard
Duration	3 hours	1–2 hours	
Repetitions	N/A	N/A	
Recovery	N/A	N/A	
Sets	N/A	N/A	
Recovery between sets	N/A	N/A	

Table 9.5 Sample sessions to train aerobic power (VO$_2$max)

Components of session	Aerobic power		Comments
	Sample 1	Sample 2	
Intensity	Sub-maximal 90% max. heart rate range	Maximal	Neither of these sessions is easy, or pain free! You should aim to ride at an intensity above normal 'race pace'. The sessions can be done over hills, or on the flat. This is an ideal stationary bike workout.
Duration	3 minutes	30 seconds	
Repetitions	3	5	
Recovery	3 minutes	30 seconds	
Sets	3	3	
Recovery between sets	5 minutes	5 minutes	

Table 9.6 *Sample sessions to train intensity threshold*

Components of session	Intensity threshold		Comments
	Sample 1	Sample 2	
Intensity	85% max. heart rate range	85–90% max. heart rate range	For this 'time trial' session, the intensity should feel 'on the edge' – any harder, and you would be unable to sustain the effort; any slower, and it would be more bearable. Again, an ideal stationary bike workout.
Duration	20 minutes	8 minutes	
Repetitions	1	3	
Recovery	N/A	4 minutes	
Sets	N/A	1	
Recovery between sets	N/A	N/A	

Table 9.7 *Sample sessions to train muscular endurance*

Components of session	Muscular endurance		Comments
	Sample 1	Sample 2	
Intensity	Maximal – high gear, low pedal speed	Maximal – high gear, low pedal speed	The effort should feel 'hard', with high resistance from the gearing and incline. As this session is more muscle-based than cardiovascular-based, you will find that your heart rate doesn't increase as high as in many of the other sessions. An ideal stationary bike workout.
Duration	20 seconds on steep hill	50 seconds on long, gradual hill	
Repetitions	6	8	
Recovery	1 minute	2 minutes	
Sets	2	1	
Recovery between sets	3 minutes	N/A	

Table 9.8 Sample sessions to train explosive power

Components of session	Explosive power		Comments
	Sample 1	Sample 2	
Intensity	Maximal sprint	Maximal, uphill sprint	The efforts should be maximal, whilst seated, in a high gear. Aim to attack each repetition aggressively, as if sprinting for the finish line. For the 6-second hill effort, you can get out of the saddle for the initial 2–3 seconds, or for the entire repetition. An ideal stationary bike workout.
Duration	10 seconds	6 seconds	
Repetitions	12	7	
Recovery	3 minutes	2 minutes	
Sets	1	2	
Recovery between sets	N/A	5 minutes of easy riding intensity	

Table 9.9 Sample sessions to train pain tolerance

Components of session	Pain tolerance		Comments
	Sample 1	Sample 2	
Intensity	Maximal	Maximal, paced effort	A very painful pair of training sessions, which should by definition be harder than any other. The biggest mistake with these sessions is starting off too hard, and being unable to maintain your 'style' or 'form'. An ideal stationary bike workout
Duration	45 seconds	90 seconds	
Repetitions	10	3	
Recovery	1 minute	3 minutes	
Sets	1	3	
Recovery between sets	N/A	6 minutes	

Table 9.10 Sample recovery session

Components of session	Recovery	Comments
Intensity	Less than 60% max. heart range	The intensity should feel light, with no discomfort experienced – almost as if it were too easy to be of benefit
Duration	Between 30 and 60 minutes	
Repetitions	N/A	
Recovery	N/A	
Sets	N/A	
Recovery between sets	N/A	

Race Preparation

How should you train as a race approaches? It's very important not to make the mistake of trying to train for a race the week before. Race fitness is developed in the *weeks* previous to an event. If you know specific details about your competitors, or about the course, you can alter your training to help you prepare as optimally as time allows. Ideally you should allow three weeks of specific preparation, and spend the week immediately prior to the event recuperating – this is known as a 'taper' week.

When you have a period free from races or tours, use your time to work on weaknesses, building up both the intensity and duration of rides. Include some hard efforts on hills, on the flat, sprinting and time trialling. Remember that you need to eat well during periods of intense training, and rest well too. During the taper week you need to refine your riding skills. Gradually reduce the training duration, while still keeping intensity relatively high – for instance, go from 25-mile to 10-mile time trials, or do half the usual number of intervals. Then, as race day approaches, ease off completely, still riding but not training. The day before, do a ride of half the race distance, with three or four 1-minute efforts at race pace.

At an event

When you get to an event, you should allow some time to look over the course – either on the bike, if it's unlikely to tire you, or in a car. Note the positioning of hills, any difficult descents and corners, and any potholes and storm covers which may cause problems. For road race reconnaissance, check where the best places will be to attack or to recover after an attack, where the wind is likely to be strongest, and on what parts of the course you can get shelter.

Make sure you eat nothing in the two hours before the event, but sip fluids up to the start time. Ensure that you warm up for at least 20, and preferably 30, minutes before the start. An ideal pre-event warm-up might be:

• 20 minutes at 65% max heart rate

• 5 × 10-second maximal sprints, with 50 seconds recovery

• 5 minutes progressing from 60% to 80% max heart rate

• race.

Afterwards

As regards your race performance, what went right or wrong, and why? Ask yourself where you lost out, what you would do differently next time, and if you can improve on anything. Be fair and try to stay clear of bringing other people into the evaluation – it is rarely other competitors that prevent you reaching a higher placing. Don't forget to look at things like your diet and sleep patterns in the days leading up to the race; these are often the cause of seemingly inexplicable poor performances.

Nutrition for competition

For advice on general nutritional principles, refer to Chapter 8, pp. 105–18.

A few days prior to a prolonged and intense competitive event, you should regulate your diet and training in an attempt to maximise or 'load' muscle glycogen stores. High pre-exercise glycogen levels will allow you to exercise harder for longer by delaying fatigue. The most practical method of glycogen loading involves training intensely to the fifth or sixth day prior to competition. During the remaining days before competition, you should gradually reduce the amount of training and eat high-carbohydrate meals (more than 600 grams) on each day of the final three days before an event. Such a regimen will increase muscle glycogen stores to 20–40 per cent above normal.

The pre-competition meal

A high-carbohydrate meal eaten within six hours of competition 'tops off' the glycogen stores in both liver and muscle. The liver, which maintains blood glucose levels, relies upon frequent meals to sustain its small stores (80–100 grams) of glycogen. Even after following a muscle glycogen loading regimen, it is wise to eat a low-fat meal containing 75–150 grams of carbohydrate three hours prior to competition. Carbohydrate consumption will vary with athletes' energy expenditure and body size. Values given for carbohydrate intake are guidelines for a 70 kg rider; they should be adjusted according to individual cyclists' needs.

During the early part of exercise, the majority of carbohydrate energy is derived from muscle glycogen. As exercise progresses, muscle glycogen is reduced and contributes less to the carbohydrate requirements of exercise. This reduced reliance upon muscle glycogen is balanced by an increased reliance upon blood glucose for carbohydrate energy. After three hours of exercise, the majority of carbohydrate energy appears to be derived from the metabolism of glucose, which is transported from the circulating blood into the exercising muscles.

After between one and three hours of continuous exercise at 70–80% of maximal oxygen uptake, cyclists will tire due to carbohydrate depletion. Carbohydrate feedings during exercise appear to delay fatigue by allowing the exercising muscles to rely mostly upon blood glucose for energy late in exercise.

After two to three hours of exercise without carbohydrate feeding, blood glucose concentration normally declines to relatively low levels. The liver reduces its output of glucose, due to depletion of liver glycogen stores, when the muscles are removing glucose from the blood at high rates. During prolonged exercise without carbohydrate feeding, fatigue may occur because insufficient blood glucose is available to compensate for the depleted muscle glycogen stores. Although a tired rider may become *hypoglycaemic* (develop low blood glucose), it is rare to experience symptoms such as light-headedness and nausea. Most riders primarily experience local muscular fatigue.

Carbohydrate feeding does not prevent fatigue; it simply delays it. During the final part of exercise, when muscle glycogen is low and athletes are relying upon blood glucose for energy, their muscles feel heavy and they must concentrate to maintain exercise at intensities that are ordinarily not stressful, when muscle glycogen stores are filled.

Consuming carbohydrate at regular intervals during prolonged, continuous exercise will ensure that sufficient carbohydrate is available during the later stages of an event. Aim for 1 gram of carbohydrate per kilogram of body weight per hour. So, a 60 kg rider should consume 60 grams of carbohydrate per hour of riding. This is most effectively achieved by using an energy drink (*see* pp. 115–16).

Appendix

Avoiding common cycling ailments

It's an unfortunate fact that the human body was not really created to sit on a bicycle. As a result, riding can cause it to suffer in a variety of ways. All common cycling ailments can, however, be alleviated by following a few sensible guidelines. *Note* Information given below relates primarily to prevention of common cycling related ailments. You should always seek professional advice from a qualified doctor or sports injury professional if in doubt, especially where a symptom persists or becomes worse despite rest.

Saddle sores

These develop when pressure and friction between shorts and skin causes chafing around the perineum (the area of the pelvic region which bears most of your bodyweight). Bacterial infections can then take hold. Prevention is better than cure, so wear only clean shorts and if necessary use a quality barrier cream. It may seem obvious, but it is important that you wash thoroughly and change into clean clothes after each cycle ride.

An ill-fitting saddle may also cause soreness. If you suspect that your saddle is to blame, get some advice from a good shop. An assistant will be able to guide you to a saddle which meets your riding needs.

If you do develop saddle sores, apply an antiseptic or anaesthetic cream – see a pharmacist for advice. Bad sores will need a course of antibiotics to clear them up.

Impotency

Sitting on a narrow, pointed seat can crush the artery that controls the ability of the penis to fill with blood. This in turn can cause impotency. Although impotency is not common, research shows that it can happen more often to cyclists than to runners.

The problem can be avoided through the use of a newer type of saddle with an oval gap; it looks something like a toilet seat. In any case, keep the saddle level, because a tilt either up or down can put more pressure on the groin. The seat height should be at a point where the rider can pedal at the bottom of the down-stroke with the leg extended but without the knee being locked out – and cyclists should lift out of the seat when going over rough areas.

Blisters

Hands and feet are susceptible to blisters and numbness. To take care of your hands, get some well-fitting cycle gloves or mitts, comfortable handlebar grips, and set up your bike properly so that you aren't putting too much weight over the front of the bike which will need to be supported by your hands. Most cycle mitts have well-padded palms which relieve pressure and can help to reduce the likelihood of vibration-related pain.

Feet can also suffer during long rides, especially when wet. Make sure shoes fit well; use some vaseline between the toes and around the heel; and get your feet warm and dry as soon as you can.

Knee pain

Knee pain is the most common cycling-related injury and is completely avoidable in nearly all cases. The causes of knee pain can range from crashes, incorrect saddle height and position, trying to push big gears while inexperienced (joints need time to adapt to repetitive actions such as pedalling), incorrect placement of the foot on the pedal, and insufficient movement of the foot on the pedal. Unavoidable knee pains are those related to diseases such as arthritis.

To avoid knee pain from the start, get help in setting up your riding position (ask a good shop or very experienced rider), and ride with your feet on the pedals in the position in which they naturally hang – some people's feet point in, some out, and some straight ahead. To check, sit on a table with your feet hanging over the edge, 8 inches apart. Relax. See how your feet point and then set up your pedals and cleats to get your feet in that position when you're on the bike. The ball of the foot should be slightly in front of the pedal axle. Inexperienced riders should limit their pedalling to higher revs – 75–90 per minute – and avoid really steep hills for a few months at least. This will prevent you from using high gears, which put considerable strain on knees.

Treat knee pain with rest, ice (three times a day) and elevate (if swollen) in the first instance. If the knee is still painful after two days see a sports injury specialist. When the pain eventually goes, ease back into training gently. Again, it's best to see a specialist for guidance relating to your particular injury.

Back pain

Cycling, and particularly mountain biking, can hurt your back. However, there are steps that can be taken to prevent low back pain. If you suffer from back pain now, go to see a specialist. Physiotherapists, osteopaths and chiropractors can help, but make sure you explain that you're a cyclist, and give them as much information as possible.

If you don't have a bad back, the best prevention is to have your bike set up properly, and to include some stretching as part of each day's activity (*see also* pp. 95–103). Effective stretching can reduce the likelihood of low back pain occurring. Occasionally sitting upright during rides will help to relieve back strain, as will changing hand positions.

Eyes

Trendy sports shades aren't just for posing – they can prevent all sorts of nasty little bits getting in your eyes. Wind, rain, dust, grime and mud can cause short-term irritation but seldom lead to serious problems. However, if you get animal 'mess' in your eye, which does happen, you could suffer from a painful eye infection – antibiotic eye drops being the usual remedy. Again, prevention is better than cure, so either wear shades or use a well-placed mudguard.

If you wear contact lenses try putting some 'tear' drops onto each lens before and after rides; these can be very refreshing and soothing.

Cramps

Cramps are an indication that you are using your muscles beyond their accustomed limit (either for a longer than normal duration, or at a higher than normal level of intensity). This explains why cramps are more common at the end of a long or particularly strenuous ride, or after an especially vigorous sprint. The pain is brought on by an intense, involuntary contraction of the muscle. Although cramps may be the result of fluid and electrolyte imbalance from sweating, that is not universally the case, as individuals involved in activities requiring chronic use of a muscle without sweating (musicians, for example) can also experience cramps.

As with other forms of activity-related muscle pain, appropriate training will decrease the possibility of cramps for any given situation or level of activity. If you are going to be exercising in excessively hot or humid conditions, pay close attention to your fluid and salt intake and add a pinch of salt to your food at these times. A sports drink might help, but it is maintaining adequate hydration which is the key.

Finally, if cramps do occur, gently stretching the affected muscle will give relief. Many believe that regular stretching will prevent cramps. A pre-ride drink of tonic water – which contains quinine – can also help.

Muscle aches
Muscle soreness is often blamed on the accumulation of waste products from exercise, primarily lactic acid. This may be true in the immediate post-exercise period, particularly when a cool-down has been skipped. However, aching muscles after exercise are primarily due to swelling of damaged muscle fibres, and can be tackled by first giving yourself a gentle massage, then getting in the bath or shower and spraying your legs with cold water. This will reduce swelling and promote blood flow through the muscle, speeding up the recovery process.

Obscure but nasty
- Ensure that you have had an anti-tetanus injection, otherwise cuts received in crashes could lead to lockjaw.

- Off-road cycling can often mean riding alongside waterways. Accidents can happen, and riders have been known to fall into rivers, streams, lakes and canals. If you develop flu symptoms after you've fallen into slow-moving or still water, go to your doctor and say where you fell. Ask to be checked for Weil's disease, which can be contracted through contact with rats' urine!

- Finally, make sure that water bottles are washed out thoroughly after every ride.

Glossary

Adenosine triphosphate (ATP) Made up of one molecule of adenosine and three phosphate molecules attached by high-energy bonds. Energy is 'trapped' inside these bonds and released to fuel movement.

Aerobic In the presence of oxygen; aerobic metabolism utilises oxygen.

Aerobic power (VO$_2$max) The maximum amount of oxygen that you can extract from the air and utilise in the working muscles for the aerobic production of energy. Also known as **aerobic capacity**.

Anaerobic Without oxygen; non-oxidation metabolism (*see* **aerobic** above).

Anaerobic threshold The point at which aerobic metabolism can no longer supply all energy needs, so that energy is produced anaerobically; indicated by an increase in **lactic acid**. Also known as lactate threshold. An important indicator of aerobic fitness.

Body composition Often considered a component of fitness; refers to the makeup of the body in terms of lean mass (muscle, bone, vital tissue and organs) relative to fat mass. An optimal ratio of fat to lean mass is an indication of fitness, and the right type of exercise will help you decrease body fat and increase or maintain muscle mass.

Calorie The commonly used unit of energy, defined as the amount of heat required to increase the temperature of 1 g of water by 1°C.

Cardiac output The volume of blood pumped by the left ventricle of the heart per minute – equals **stroke volume** multiplied by heart rate.

Cardiorespiratory system Heart, blood and blood vessels, and lungs.

Cardiovascular system Heart, blood and blood vessels.

Cardiovascular training A level of **aerobic** exercise that taxes the **cardiovascular system** enough to stimulate physiological adaptation – such that it is able to deliver and utilise oxygen sufficiently to fuel prolonged intensive exercise.

Cholesterol A form of fat that is ingested in the diet and is also produced in the liver. A high level of cholesterol, and especially a high ratio of total cholesterol to low-density lipoproteins, is associated with increased risk of coronary heart disease.

Circuit training A series of different exercises completed one after the other that are varied in intervals. One of the most time-efficient workouts because you accomplish more activities within less time.

Conditioning Activities that exercise the whole body to improve overall physical fitness, especially aerobic fitness, **musclular strength** and **endurance**, and flexibility.

Cycle ergometer A stationary bike that is calibrated and produces measurable units of work, such that a cyclist's **power** output can be measured.

Duration The length of time of a given workout.

Endurance The ability of a muscle or group of muscles to overcome a resistance for an extended period of time, and repeatedly. The ability to resist fatigue. Also known as stamina.

Enzymes Complex proteins formed in living cells which assist chemical processes without being changed themselves, i.e. organic catalysts.

Explosive power The ability to develop near-maximal tone in a very short time.

Flexibility The ability to move joints and use muscles through their full range of motion.

Frequency The number of times per week that one trains.

Fast glycolytic muscle fibres (FG) Muscle fibres that are well adapted for **anaerobic** respiration and reach peak tension very quickly.

Fast oxidative glycolytic muscle fibres (FOG) Similar to **fast glycolytic fibres** but with training they are capable of adapting to **aerobic** respiration.

Glucose Simple sugar.

Glycogen The form in which **glucose** is stored in the muscles and liver.

Haemoglobin The iron-containing pigment of red blood cells that carries oxygen around the body to the working muscles.

Hormones Chemical messengers produced by the body and transported in the blood to the target tissue.

Insulin Hormone produced by the pancreas, and used in carbohydrate **metabolism** and transportation of glucose to the working muscles.

Intensity The level of work, or how hard one is working.

Intensity threshold Also called 'onset of blood lactate accumulation (OBLA)', or **lactate threshold**. The workload at which lactate production is greater than lactate removal; lactate builds up to a level which interferes with muscular contraction.

Interval training Consists of intermittent exercise with regular rest periods. The ratio of work to rest is manipulated according to the desired training effect.

Lactic acid A by-product of intense exercise. This can build-up in the muscle – blocking muscle contraction, causing a burning sensation, and eventually forcing the body to slow down.

Lactate threshold *See* **anaerobic threshold**.

Lactate tolerance The body's ability to tolerate **lactic acid** build-up.

Maximum heart rate The maximum heart rate possible for an individual during any given exercise modality.

Maximum heart rate reserve (MHRR) True **maximum heart rate** minus true **resting heart rate**.

Maximum oxygen uptake (VO_2max) *See* **aerobic power**.

Metabolic rate (metabolism) The rate at which your body burns **calories**.

Mitochondria The 'powerhouse' of the cell. A structure within the cells that has the specific function of making energy in the form of ATP.

Muscular endurance The ability of a muscle or group of muscles to exert force to overcome a resistance, repeatedly and for an extended period of time.

Muscular strength An expression of the amount of force generated by one single, maximum contraction. Refers to the ability of a muscle or group of muscles to exert maximum force to overcome a resistance.

Myoglobin A protein found in muscle that transports oxygen from the cell membrane to the mitochondria (which generate energy within the cell).

Overload A training load that challenges the body's current level of fitness.

Pain tolerance The ability to continue a high work rate while suffering discomfort in the propulsive muscles.

Periodisation A method of structuring training in order to prevent over-training and to optimise peak performance.

Power The product of force and velocity, or **strength** x speed.

Progression Increasing **overload** at just the right rate to result in fitness gains.

Rate of perceived exertion (RPE) Rates the **intensity** of exercise by how hard it feels.

Repetitions Number of times an exercise is repeated.

Resting heart rate (RHR) Heart rate taken in the morning after waking up (gently), emptying the bladder and then resting again for a few minutes to allow the heart rate to settle.

Sets A group of exercises performed in **repetitions** and separated by a recovery period.

Slow oxidative muscle fibres (SO) Muscle fibres which have a lot of mitochondria and oxidative enzymes and a plentiful supply of capillaries. They are well adapted for **aerobic** respiration.

Specificity A principle of training which dictates that in order to improve a certain component of fitness or in a given activity, a person must train specifically for that component or activity.

Strength The force that a muscle or group of muscles can exert against a resistance.

Stroke volume The amount of blood ejected from the left ventricle per heart beat.

Taper Reduction in training levels to ensure that an athlete is fresh for a competitive event.

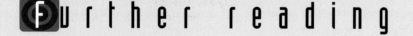

Further reading

Armstrong, Lance and Carmichael, Chris and Nye, Joffre (2000) *The Lance Armstrong Performance Program*, (Emmaus, PA: Rodale Press).

Boardman, Chris (2000) *The Complete Book of Cycling*, (Partridge Press).

Burke, Edmund, R. (1998) *Cycling Health and Physiology: Using Sports Science to Improve Your Riding and Racing*, 2nd edn, (Chambersburg, PA: Vitesse Press).

Edwards, S. and Reed, S. (2000) *The Heart Rate Monitor Log Book for Outdoor and Indoor Cyclists: A Heart Zone Training Programme*, (Boulder, Colarado: Velo Press).

Pavelka, Edward, (Ed.) (2000) *Bicycling Magazine's Nutrition for Peak Performance: Eat and Drink for Maximum Energy on the Road and Off*, (Emmaus, PA: Rodale Press).

Index

Page numbers in **bold** type refer to table and diagrams, those in *italics* refer to illustrations.